MORE THAN SORRY

MORE THAN SORRY

5 STEPS TO DEEPEN YOUR APOLOGY AFTER
YOU HAVE COMMITTED INFIDELITY

DR. DEBORAH S. MILLER, LPC

More Than Sorry: 5 Steps to Deepen Your Apology After You Have Committed Infidelity

Library of Congress Control Number: 2021392190

ISBN: 978-1-7369820-0-6 (ebook) | ISBN 978-1-7369820-1-3 (paperback)

*This book is dedicated to my husband of 45 years,
Mark Miller.
I am grateful for his unfailing support, love, compassion, and
forgiveness. Thank you.*

THERE'S A HOLE IN MY SIDEWALK: THE ROMANCE OF SELF-DISCOVERY

BY PORTIA NELSON

"I walk down the street.
There is a deep hole in the sidewalk.
I fall in.
I am lost... I am helpless.
It isn't my fault.
It takes forever to find a way out.

I walk down the same street.
There is a deep hole in the sidewalk.
I pretend I don't see it.
I fall in again.
I can't believe I am in the same place.
But it isn't my fault.
It still takes me a long time to get out.

I walk down the same street.
There is a deep hole in the sidewalk.
I see it is there.
I still fall in. It's a habit.

My eyes are open.
I know where I am.
It is my fault. I get out immediately.
I walk down the same street.
There is a deep hole in the sidewalk.
I walk around it.
I walk down another street."

CONTENTS

FIND THE COURAGE TO START

INTRODUCTION

Sometimes it takes a painful experience to make us change our ways.

GNB Proverbs 20:30

You crossed the line in your relationship. You secretly became involved with someone else. You regret your offense, and you want to move forward. But your partner still needs to talk about it and needs to hear more than "I'm sorry." They want to know "Why, why did you hurt those who love you? Why weren't you honest about your feelings? The questions are fair, but your answers are weak. "I don't know" is insufficient but often accurate.

This book is for you – the person who had an extramarital affair or who had a secret online relationship. *More Than Sorry* offers a blueprint for self-examination where you will gain more clarity about your "why." Take the steps outlined here to explore your infidelity, deepen your apology, and repair relationships. Starting this journey is a courageous act.

As a licensed professional counselor in private practice, I worked for over 20 years with couples dealing with the aftermath of affairs. They came to my office with different goals – some wanted to mend their relationship, others wanted questions answered, and others wanted to figure out how to end their partnership. I have worked with couples who repaired and strengthened their relationships through conversations that exposed emotional vulnerability and asserted a shared commitment to their future. Sadly, I have also worked with those who felt that their emotional scars were too deep and chose to end their partnership. I have also experienced the "return" couples who couldn't get past the affair and needed to revisit it years after the affair ended.

Usually, repair work with couples focuses heavily on supporting the wounded partner who needs to vent their anger, shock, fears, and sadness. During these intense emotional counseling sessions, the betrayer typically sits silently with their feelings of sadness, shame, and anxiety. Because the victim's pain is so significant, it is tempting to focus only on them and to ignore the adulterer. If the goal for recovery is forgiveness, then the betrayer must find ways to deepen his/her apology, accept responsibility for the dishonesty, and share more authentically about their inner world. *Healing for both the individual and the couple cannot happen without honesty, self-analysis, and exploration of the affair.* I call this process "navel gazing."

Tom and Chloe came to me for affair recovery. He was seemingly remorseful about his year-long relationship with a co-worker, yet verbally inadequate in his apology. Tom appeared tongue-tied, voicing halting apologies for the affair and stating ignorance about "why." He was sick of the questions and thought his reassurance that he wouldn't continue the secret relationship was enough to stop the redundant discussion.

Tom resisted the introspective work I prescribed to him – the same tasks offered to you. He was hesitant, unwilling to start self-analysis, and he feared pain, embarrassment, frustration, and heightened shame. His defense mechanisms were on high alert as he worked to minimize, deflect, and explain the transgression. Stating an apology, such as "I'm sorry. It won't happen again," was somewhat helpful, but it was not enough to heal the hurt of infidelity. I explained to Tom that he would have to look in the mirror and face his inglorious mistakes to repair the damage and move forward in a healthy relationship.

More Than Sorry illustrates Tom and four other individuals' navel-gazing journey who worked to deepen their apology to their spouses and families. With each couple, the outcome varied in their success. You will find, in their relatable stories, inspiration and commonality.

You may have found *More Than Sorry* on your own, but it is more likely that it was given to you by someone hurt by your violation of trust. Whether you feel intrinsically or extrinsically motivated, find the energy to use this tool to start the repair journey now. Taking no action to make amends is irresponsible. It is time to embrace yourself as a mature adult who can and will be open and honest and who will intentionally work to make a change. You have hurt others, and as much as you want them to forgive and forget, you know it can't happen without diving into your betrayals. A courageous, intensive self-examination, coupled with profound empathy and compassion for those hurt by your betrayal will lead to heightened self-respect and healthier relationships in the future.

From my work with many couples, I know that healing can happen. I know that forgiveness can happen. Although the journey of navel gazing is exhausting and at times draining, trust that looking at yourself honestly will lead to more intimate and authentic relationships with others. The goal is to own your guilt about your choices, make amends, and authentically change. Hopefully, others will forgive you after you take action to deepen your apology through honest connections. The bonus of this work is that you will discover new parts of yourself that will enhance your self-love and self-forgiveness. You will become more assertive in knowing that *your past sins don't have to define who you are today and in the future.*

Your betrayal story is one that doesn't have an ending but reflects the peaks and valleys of being human. Your reflections can reveal sin, redemption, change, and growth. Past experiences and relationships are building blocks of who you are now and who you will be in the future.

Answering the "Why?" of your affair is a challenging

journey to do singularly. Your defense mechanisms mask seeing an honest reflection in the mirror and acceptance of your actions and wrongdoings. Talking to a therapist or a friend who can stay objective and supportive can help you process your affair more deeply and help you discover more honest answers that lay beneath your "I don't know why I did it; I'm sorry" response. Enlist a partner to ensure your accountability for sticking with the self-exploration.

How long will this process of self-examination take, you ask? The navel-gazing process should take about four to six weeks if you follow the prompts spelled out in this workbook. Pace the work to allow time to process all of your thoughts and feelings. I recommend tackling each chapter every three to four days. Do not complete the whole book in one sitting. Determine where and when you will be the most successful in doing the work. Is it in your office? Your kitchen? At a coffee shop? At night? First thing in the morning? Set up space and the routine. Between the work, take breaks from talking about your affair. Play, have fun, and focus on other things like family, friends, your career, and exercise. But do come back to the navel-gazing work.

The goal of *More Than Sorry* is to initiate a lifelong practice of self-awareness, journaling, mindfulness, empathy, and compassion, along with the courage and skills to periodically check in with yourself and your partner to revisit the affair. This navel-gazing work will build your commitment to make healthier choices and to grow personally. You can grow from your infidelity crisis, find joy, and live life with a vengeance! You can feel lighter and less burdened with guilt. You can build your self-respect.

Reflect on these questions found in the journal prompts:

- Do you WANT to be forgiven?
- Do you know WHY you want to receive forgiveness?
- Do you know HOW to ask for forgiveness?

Perhaps you:

- Want forgiveness and to regain self-respect.
- Want to repair relationships.
- Recognize the depth of others' pain.
- Want to affirm that you can change.
- Want to be courageous in owning your mistakes.
- Want to accept your humanness.

I'm challenging you to embrace the following call to action: "I don't know exactly why I chose to have an affair, but I'm going to spend time looking deeper into my wrongdoing. I commit to this navel-gazing process to strengthen my empathy for those I have hurt and for myself. I will say out loud to myself and at least one other person what I'm discovering. Now and in the future, I will try my best to do what is right."

JOURNAL PROMPT
WHY?

Why am I starting this introspective work? What do I hope to gain?

_____

_____

_____

_____

What are my fears in starting this work?

_____

_____

_____

_____

Do I want to be forgiven? Why?

_____

_____

_____

_____

Do I know how to ask for forgiveness?

_____

_____

_____

_____

To whom do I want to ask forgiveness?

_____

_____

_____

_____

What outcomes am I hoping for at the end of this navel-gazing work?

_____

_____

_____

_____

SAY IT OUT LOUD. SHARE YOUR THOUGHTS WITH A TRUSTED FRIEND OR MENTAL HEALTH PROFESSIONAL.

GLOSSARY OF TERMS

I am using specific labels throughout this book to keep the discussion clear and free from gender bias and judgment.

The AFFAIR: This refers to your secret relationship with another person, either in person, online (i.e., social media sites, email, texting), or through online pornography sites.

The NAVEL-GAZER: This is you who had an affair or secret relationship. For some, the term navel gazing may suggest a selfish, self-absorbed individual who ignores others' needs. In the context of this work, a navel- gazer thinks deeply about their transgression.

The WOUNDED: This is the person you hurt and betrayed and who suffered the most from your secret relationship.

The OTHER: This is with whom the physical and emotional transgression happened. This label refers to a person or an online pornography site.

The FAMILY: This refers to your children, other family members, and friends who may or may not know about the outside relationship.

MEET THE COUPLES

W oven throughout this book are stories of five couples who attempt relationship recovery through navel gazing. While fictional, these couples are a compilation of real clients seen in my practice over the years. All of the navel gazers are somewhat remorseful but are in emotional pain, unsure of their willingness to work on repair, resist self-examination, and strive to protect their egos. All contend with understanding the "Why?" of their affair, and all struggle with reaching forgiveness. The wounded all share feelings of betrayal, anger, hurt and distrust in their partner's attempts at restitution. Notice how you identify with their challenges.

Tom and Chloe had been married for 11 years and had two school-aged children. Tom was highly involved with his children, his family of origin, and his church. He coached softball teams, attended Bible study, and was supportive of his aging parents. He was a busy man who spent little time at home. Before discovering her husband's year-long affair with a co-worker, Chloe's main complaint was that Tom was too busy and they did not spend enough time together as a couple. Their marriage lacked physical and emotional intimacy. Frequent verbal arguments and long periods of silence were the norm. When she stumbled onto a voicemail revealing his secret relationship, she barraged Tom with lots of questions in an attempt to discover the truth about his affair. Angered by the interrogations, he increasingly avoided time at home and ignored demands to quit working with the other. Chloe struggled with regaining her trust in her husband and suspected he was lying when he said that the affair was over. The counseling sessions, where she vented her anger and hurt, were dramatic and emotional. Chloe would scream, cry, and repeat over and over her hurt and shock. In response, Tom would stare at his feet, roll his eyes, verbally shut down, get angry, and avoid answering questions. With frustration, he repeatedly stated, "I'm sorry. The affair is over." He did not understand the need to rehash details about his romance. He hated the barrage of questions. Consequently, he frequently made excuses to miss therapy sessions.

Carmen and Elena had been together for five years. They enjoyed a rich social life and extensive travel. Excited to have a baby, Carmen chose to put her music career on hold to be a stay-at-home mom with their infant daughter. To maintain their lifestyle, Elena committed to long hours in a stressful job that left her depleted upon returning home. Their typical evening included a quick dinner, the routine of putting their baby to bed, and a ten-minute adult conversation before they collapsed for the night at 9:00 p.m. Carmen felt trapped at home, was bored and isolated. Social media filled the void and she connected with other stay-at-home moms through Facebook. She chatted at least four hours a day with one friend in particular, and they became very close and emotionally intimate. Initially, their relationship was platonic, but increasingly, they became more flirtatious and affectionate. Carmen looked forward to their daily contact and didn't share the importance of the friendship with her partner. The secret relationship became more and more time-consuming. Elena knew of the other but didn't see the depth of their connection until she discovered Carmen's open Facebook conversations. Elena was angry and hurt. She had blamed the lack of intimacy in their marriage on mutual exhaustion. Now she understood the prolonged silences. Carmen was defensive when the online affair was exposed. She struggled to understand how this friendship was considered an affair and a violation of their marriage vows of commitment. She had not physically met the other and they had no plans for a rendezvous.

Tasha and Eric were married for 30 years. They had no history of significant struggles, and they described their relationship as financially and socially comfortable. Both had satisfying careers and were seemingly content in leading their parallel lives with some intersections of time with their children, grandchildren, and aging parents. Historically, Tasha had lots of energy for taking care of others, doing volunteer work, and keeping busy socially. Her community saw her as generous and energetic. At her 35th high school reunion, she reconnected with an old boyfriend, and they started a publicly open relationship. Eric was completely blindsided. He had always trusted his wife and assumed they were happy, content, and committed. When he confronted her, she said indignantly, "It is my time to have some fun"!

William and Kim had only been married a couple of years, and their relationship had multiple challenges. As a couple, they prided themselves on being aware of and accepting each other's emotional and financial challenges. They had two small children, were in debt, and lived paycheck-to-paycheck. Kim received disability benefits due to her mental health struggles. Her struggles with Bipolar Disorder and Anxiety Disorders compounded her feelings of isolation and anxiety as a stay-at-home mom. She was aware that, before marriage, William was addicted to pornography and visited online erotica sites daily. She recognized that his night-shift work contributed to his fatigue, stress, and detachment from the family, but the discovery that he was secretly on several pay-for-porn sites made her furious! Her belief that they were totally open and honest with each other was shattered. Although he voiced remorse, his attempts to quit pornography were not successful, and he hid his relapses.

Bruce and Carlos had been together for 15 years and described their relationship as healthy, characterized by a strong friendship and good sexual connection. Five years before their first therapy session, they publicly declared their monogamy in a commitment ceremony. They were also attempting to adopt a baby. Bruce traveled for work and was out of town at least five days per month. Emails and financial statements revealed that Bruce had, over the past year, multiple one-night stands while away from home. Carlos was sickened and embarrassed by the affairs and fell into a deep depression. The couple separated for a few months before starting couple's therapy to explore reconciliation.

———

Reflect on the descriptions of these five couples and the similarities with your situation. Continue to read and experience their navel-gazing journeys throughout More Than Sorry. *Find, in their struggles, motivation and inspiration to continue the path to deepening your apology.*

STEP ONE: HEAL THROUGH EMPATHY

COMMUNICATE EMPATHY FOR THE WOUNDED

You broke your partner's heart. Do you know this at a deep, visceral level? You must intellectually and emotionally understand the depth of the pain and validate the hurt they have experienced. Can you put yourself in their shoes and connect with their angst? Those wounded by your secret relationship may suffer deep scars in their self-esteem, confidence, and sense of security. The first step to repair your relationships is communicating empathy which is the basic building block for rebuilding a connection. It is time to be authentically curious about what the wounded is feeling and thinking. The challenge is to be fully present and to listen without defensiveness to all of their emotions. When faced with the ramifications of your infidelity, your first instinct will be to run and avoid the reflection of yourself as a betrayer. But don't! Plant your feet, be remorseful, take responsibility, and show courage to listen openly.

Chloe, Elena, Eric, Kim, and Carlos were all blindsided by their partners' betrayals. To work through their shock, they needed to ask many questions and vent a wide range of emotions. In each of their homes, there were bouts of hysteria, screaming, non-stop tears, silence, avoidance, physical and verbal attacks. The rehashing of the affair was intense and exhausting for both parties. Like Tom, Carmen, Tasha, William, and Bruce, you have to challenge the urge to retreat into your pain and defensiveness when faced with intense emotions and accusations. To support your partner and deepen the apology for the affair, you, the navel-gazer have to understand, learn, and practice the skill of empathy.

Communicating empathy is more complex than it sounds. *It takes courage and skill to validate and listen without defensiveness and judgment.* You will be listening to intense pain – pain that you inflicted. Due to the shame associated with telling others about the betrayal, your significant other will likely rely on you for answers and emotional support. At the same time, they will continue to direct their anger, pain, and sadness at you. Stay strong. Be present, patient, and stay calm. Don't turn your back on those you have hurt. When listening to their pain, your first inclination will be to offer advice. This advice is often unwanted. It is essential to clarify that your partner needs your support, but not your advice. Let me repeat this: the wounded does not want your advice.

What is wanted is for you, the listener, to understand, support, and acknowledge that yes, it is awful that they feel so bad. Communicate that you own how your choices have caused anger, depression, mistrust, and embarrassment. Discouraged by the wounded's need to ask more and more questions, you may get frustrated with how often you must listen to the descriptions of pain, fears, anger, and mistrust. Your defensiveness will bubble up. While keeping the focus on the wounded, the goal is to manage your frustration, anger, and avoidance. It is essential for you, the navel gazer, to stay engaged and to communicate empathy, a two-fold process:

1. You must sense what the other person is feeling. Empathy is the ability to name explicitly and implicitly expressed emotions. Hear what words are said and what their body language is communicating.

2. You must verbally validate and reflect on the other person's experience. Use words to say, "I get it" or "I'm trying to get it." Acknowledge the information shared in addition to how they are speaking and acting. Validate comments made and comment on body language, tone and pitch of voice, and facial expressions.

Having an expanded emotion vocabulary is needed to say out loud what you sense the other person is expressing. Typically, we only recognize three basic emotions – sad, mad, and glad. These three words are limited in acknowledging the full range of emotional experience.

Now, find the words to deepen the reflection of someone's sadness. Think of the different degrees of sorrow one can feel. To accurately validate, you might sense and verbalize one of the following emotional descriptors: upset, feeling down, devastated, immobilized, heavy, tearful, or depressed. See how powerful these words are in empathizing with the other person's experience? Do the same exercise finding different descriptors of 'mad.' Richer synonyms might be one of the following: upset, hurt, irritated, enraged, or devastated. Now practice with more robust validation of 'glad.' What words can you think of that might fall somewhere between 'pleased' or 'ecstatic'? Note that there is always an overlap of emotions. Humans don't typically feel just one emotion at a time. For example, anger masks fear; tears can express happiness, frustration, and exhaustion; rage interlaces with insecurities.

The challenge is to expand your emotional vocabulary. Throughout the day, notice what you are feeling and name it verbally. The more practice you have at identifying your internal feelings, the easier it will be to recognize others' sentiments. What three emotions are you experiencing right now? I challenge you to stop, reflect and identify your feelings. Perhaps you feel discouraged, overwhelmed, angry, or bored.

Besides verbally communicating empathy, your body language and tone of voice are powerful in showing interest and understanding. To show that you are curious, and empathetic, face the person speaking, keep your body open (no crossed arms), and maintain eye contact. Watch your tone of voice and try to stay calm and relaxed. Yes, this is hard to do in the face of intense anger and sorrow. Beware of being hooked into a strong emotional reaction. Remember to stay strong, present, patient, and stay calm. Don't turn your back on those you have hurt.

Let me emphasize that *communicating empathy is a skill that you can learn through study and practice.* I suggest that you work with the following format wherein you verbally validate the wounded's feelings:

> "I am hearing that you are feeling (name the emotion – anger, hurt, sad, worry, shock, etc.) because (name the situation)."

Examples of empathetic responses are:

- "You are furious at me because I kept secrets for so long."
- "You feel depressed because I did so many things that betrayed our relationship."
- "You are feeling discouraged about our future together because I have broken your trust."
- "You hate me because I cheated."

I suggest that you reflect on the wounded's feelings three times before defending yourself or asking questions. This skill is hard to put into practice but practice you must. The typical human reaction to listening to deep pain and anger is minimizing, deflecting, explaining, and defending. But believe me, this two-step communication of empathy works! Through validation, you say that you understand, respect, and accept what your partner is going through. While finding the right words to communicate empathy is helpful, it can also sound a bit robotic if not coupled with your authentic emotional connection. You need to have a level of awareness within yourself and an ability to recognize the emotions in others. Tom struggled with communicating empathy to Chloe, as did William since both had a minimal emotional vocabulary and self-awareness. They both strained to identify emotions expressed by their partners and had difficulty articulating the feelings expressed. When faced with tears and anger, both Tom and William were defensive and angry. They didn't attempt to understand their own emotions, much less those expressed by their partner. They said "sorry" multiple times but never mastered the skill of empathy, leaving all parties feeling irritated at the lack of support and understanding.

Able to calmly listen with sincerity and remorse to Carlos's pain and shock, Bruce stayed present and attentive for the long discussions about his betrayals. He kept his defensiveness at bay to support and validate all of his partner's thoughts and feelings. Repeatedly he said, "I know you are shocked and angry that I cheated. I guess you are not sure you can ever trust me again when I go out of town. You must be so angry that I chose to betray your trust. It is hard for you to believe me that I do love you and want to stay in our marriage." Over time, Bruce and Carlos's conversations held less anger, more mutual curiosity, and willingness to work together toward change.

A strong signal that validation is needed is when a person keeps repeating themselves. If they sound like a broken record, they don't think you have honestly heard or understood what was said. Even if you disagree with the wounded, you can still validate their thoughts and feelings. After communicating empathy, the injured will reciprocate and listen. Here is an illustration:

> Elena: "How could you deliberately sabotage our family? You ignored our child and me when you spent so much time with your new friend!"
>
> Carmen: "I'm hearing that you feel like I abandoned you and our child. You are angry that I spent so much time with my new friend at your expense, and you feel like I prioritized her over our family. You are angry that I kept such a big secret."

After a series of at least three empathetic statements, Carmen can then say how she feels.

> Carmen: "I didn't realize that my online friendship was a betrayal of your trust. My secret relationship grew out of my boredom and isolation, and I'm sorry I hurt you. I didn't realize that I was paying less attention to our family. I thought I was doing a good job taking care of our child and the household."

Hopefully, Elena has also learned the skill of validation and can communicate empathy. Ideally, there is a back-and-forth exchange where both parties get to say how they feel and know that the other is trying to listen and understand.

The magic of validation is that once one feels heard, the emotional intensity lessens, and one will then be able to calm down emotionally. Unexpressed or stuffed emotions metastasize. Sometimes we need to throw a bit of a temper tantrum and vent big emotions even though we know we aren't rational. Allowing others to express their feelings while you communicate remorse is a critical piece of the healing process. *Accepting all the wounded's emotions is an act of unconditional love and respect.* William had to take Kim's rage, her screaming, and her silence. He had to validate and repeatedly empathize with her anger and hurt before she could reduce the heightened emotions. It was only after extensive venting of her feelings, coupled with hearing validation and remorse, that Kim could begin to problem-solve steps toward marriage recovery.

The wounded will experience a range of emotions. Initially, they will likely be in denial, followed by feelings of confusion and shock. The realization that the affair happened to them personally will just feel unacceptable. Chloe, like Eric and Carmen, all wondered, "Why me?" They all felt like their partner's secret relationship wasn't fair. The wounded were doing what one should be doing in a relationship – supporting the family, assuming trust, and accepting the ups and downs in their partnership. They all felt the injustice of the betrayer's choice and felt victimized. The wounded did not choose this pain. Use your empathy skills.

The wounded's reactions can include anger, shame, sadness, and protective numbness. This emotional pain can cloud the brain, leading to poor concentration and forgetfulness. Chloe had difficulty functioning at home since her emotions were so intense and hindered her ability to work, do errands, and take care of their home and family. To cope, she isolated herself. The children were confused by all of the drama and physical and emotional absence of their parents.

Kim, like Chloe, felt intense emotions, primarily depression and anger. They both had bouts of uncontrollable crying and rage. Experiencing all of these heightened emotions left them feeling exhausted both physically and emotionally. Remember, you, the navel gazer, can't stop the feelings expressed by others. Your job is to validate and support through the use of your empathy skills.

The wounded may feel their self-esteem shatter and feel inadequate, insignificant, and unlovable. Kim blamed herself for William's choice to use online pornography sites. She was self-critical – assuming that her mental health challenges drove him to the computer for secret relationships.

Eric also experienced a drop in his self-esteem. Watching his wife, Tasha, be so happy and public in her other relationship intensified his self-doubt and spiraled him into feelings of inadequacy and low self-worth. Friends noticed his isolation, low energy, and loss of interest in activities he previously enjoyed. When your partner experiences these feelings, use your empathy skills.

Carlos was stuck on trying to understand what happened. He asked the same questions repeatedly. "How many times did you have sex with others?" "Did you think about me at all when you were cheating?" Bruce was frustrated by the repetitive, persistent, and somewhat redundant queries focusing on the hookups' quality and frequency. Like most wounded, Carlos fixated on the specifics of the affair. Vivid images of his partner having sex with anonymous people repeatedly played in his brain, and he was obsessed with knowing every detail. Bruce worked to use his empathy skills.

Expect suspicion since you have lost the trust of your partner. At first, Carlos and Carmen didn't believe that they heard the whole truth from their respective partners. They mandated passwords to access all electronic communications, email, social media sites, phone, and bank records. They needed verification that the cheater had stopped outside relationships, was genuinely remorseful, and tried to make significant changes. You must validate your breach of trust and reassure, through your navel-gazing, that your cheating behaviors have stopped. Instead of getting defensive and protective of your privacy, use your empathy skills.

The wounded will likely have few if any, confidants to help them through this recovery process. All of the injured in these case studies were embarrassed to reach out to family and friends for support. They feared judgment and shame from others and didn't want to set themselves up to be the target of gossip. Sharing the betrayal with others typically leads to strong advice-giving, which may or may not be helpful. Friends and family often are quick to suggest that you, the cheater, get kicked out of the home.

Consequently, Chloe, Kim, Carlos, Carmen, and Eric all felt lonely and isolated. Acknowledge that you, the betrayer, are also unwilling to tell your community about your affair for many the same reasons of shame and embarrassment. Even though you also feel lonely, isolated, and not supported, your first job is to help the wounded. Let me emphasize this –*validating the betrayed is the priority in making amends.* Use your empathy skills.

Somatic symptoms are typical in this highly emotional state. Sleep and appetite will be affected, as well as other physical aches like headaches and an upset digestive system. Emotional stress plays havoc on the physical body. Kim asked her medical doctors to adjust her mood stabilizers in light of the porn-site discovery drama. Carlos dropped 10 pounds from loss of appetite and could sleep no more than four hours a night for some time. While using your empathy skills, evaluate if your partner needs medical support during this heightened emotional time.

Be aware of your partner's emotional triggers from events, items, particular dates, TV shows, songs, and locations. Carlos was distraught each time Bruce had out-of-town work obligations. Elena felt uncomfortable each time she saw Carmen on the computer. TV shows about infidelity emotionally triggered Chloe. Eric relived the pain from the betrayal each time he drove by the high school where his wife had reconnected with her old flame. Kim was intensely emotional each time she saw their bank statement in the mailbox. You must understand that triggers can remain active for the wounded's entire life. If you notice that the injured is upset by something, acknowledge it out loud and use your empathy skills. Your repair work coupled with time will lead to diminished emotional reactions to triggered memories.

Your partner may refuse physical contact and sex. Ask permission to touch them and accept that this is their choice – a choice you must honor. Be aware that the wounded may suffer intrusive thoughts or mental images of you and your affair partner during lovemaking, which may cause an emotional shutdown or elevate extreme emotions like anger and sadness. Sex is not the only avenue to intimacy. With permission from the wounded, a simple hug, handholding, and kisses coupled with a reiteration of your sincere apology can go a long way in the healing process. Use your empathy skills to validate how the images of sex with the other are vivid and hurtful.

Carmen and Bruce could listen, feel compassion, and allow their partners to express their fears, anger, and sadness without pushing back with excuses. They sincerely communicated empathy and provided validation for all the pain expressed. Consequently, intimacy returned.

Resist the urge to be the cheerleader and provide pep talks that inadvertently minimize the wounded's feeling of hopelessness. The fear that they can never trust you or others again nor experience peace and joy is real. They will feel discouraged that comprehensive repair and recovery is not possible in your relationship. As much as you would like to talk them out of this pessimism, you must use your empathy skills to validate and support their here-and-now feelings. *Be present; don't judge nor give advice. Just listen and empathize.*

I'm challenging you to embrace the following call to action: "I don't know exactly why I chose to have an affair, but I'm going to spend time looking deeper into my wrongdoing. I commit to this navel-gazing process to strengthen my empathy for those I have hurt and for myself. I will say out loud to myself and at least one other person what I'm discovering. Now and in the future, I will try my best to do what is right."

JOURNAL PROMPT
EMPATHY FOR THE WOUNDED

Have a conversation with the wounded. Explore how they feel about your affair, be curious and verbally validate their answers to the following questions:

———————

How did you feel about me during the affair, at the discovery, and now?

_____

_____

_____

_____

How did you feel about yourself during the affair, at the discovery, and now?

_____

_____

_____

_____

What triggers you into reliving the pain (e.g., sights, smells, TV, movies)?

_____

_____

_____

What makes it difficult for you to forgive me? What are your roadblocks?

_____

_____

_____

What happens to you when I try to answer your questions?

_____

_____

_____

What do you need from me today? Is it okay if I touch you? Hug you? Hold hands?

_____

_____

_____

Add your own interview questions.

———

Say it OUT LOUD. Share your thoughts with a trusted friend or mental health professional.

FIND EMPATHY FOR YOURSELF

A s discussed, it is imperative to listen, validate, and empathize with the wounded. But you, as a human, also need to be supported as you start this repair journey. *More Than Sorry* will push you to dissect your experience in the affair and recognize that you, too, are struggling with a range of feelings, thoughts, and physical effects. It likely shakes you to the core to realize that others perceive you as an evil person who knowingly hurt others. You may feel depressed, angry, defensive, isolated, full of shame and hopelessness. You may experience somatica symptoms, such as erratic sleep and abdominal issues.

Yes, you are human. Universally, we all need validation, support, and to be seen and heard. You need empathy to find the energy to do this challenging work. Remember, empathy is different from sympathy – of which you are currently receiving little. Yes, you inflicted, through your choices, pain on others, but you must find the balance between the recriminations and self-love and respect.

Acknowledge that your ego is working hard to defend your choices and identity. *Accept your infidelity and muster up courage, curiosity, and humility to own your wrongdoings while resisting being consumed with shame.* Challenge the perception that you won't change and work toward a new reality of growth, a more authentic self, and a more profound apology for your affair.

Your inner dialogue may vacillate between, "I'm a terrible person who doesn't deserve forgiveness, and I am generally a good person who contributes to my family and society." "I am a selfish person, and I accept my humanness and mistakes and will repent and change". "I don't deserve happiness, and I deserve a second chance."

Accept the internal conflict and dichotomies. *All humans can simultaneously act and feel in two opposing ways.* For example, your secret relationship hurt others, and you may have been a good parent or church member at the same time. You may feel lots of shame for your transgression, and you may feel proud of your successes. You may like and dislike your affair partner. You may like and despise your significant other. You feel energized to work toward restitution, and you feel hopeless. Self-empathy mandates that you listen to yourself, fully accepting all your dichotomous feelings to set a course for change.

Apply the two-fold process of empathy skills to yourself:

1. Identify your feelings.

2. Verbally validate all your thoughts and feelings. Express all your experiences to another person or in your journals.

Acknowledge feelings of insecurity around the wounded. Intimacy, physically and emotionally, is probably a struggle. As the betrayer, you may repress complaints about your partner. Acknowledge all your feelings in your journal and perhaps to a neutral confidante, to release your fears, anger, hurt, and confusion. You may still have strong feelings for the other. You may worry and feel a bit protective of them. Ironically, the secretiveness of that relationship may have deepened your connection and attachment. The two of you shared multiple highs and lows. Thus, you will grieve, at some level, the end of that relationship. It is essential to empathize with all your feelings, at least to yourself, to manage them and, hopefully, release them.

Tom was confident, respected, positive, and energized at work, where he felt worthy, accepted, and sexually attracted to the other. He was resentful of his wife and was sullen, irritable, and disinterested in his family's lives. He needed to explore his experiences at work and home with curiosity. Initially, the challenge was to empathize with his conflicting feelings and behavior and articulate them with the hope of finding clarity.

It was easy for Carmen to recognize that she felt isolated and lonely as a stay-at-home mom. She felt guilt and remorse over her secret relationship while also intimately connected with her online friend. She struggled to accept all her feelings and felt discouraged about finding future happiness. Receiving empathy for these emotions helped to lift her energy to address her problems.

Tasha felt both content and rebellious in her marriage. Processing her feelings with curiosity, she empathized with her loneliness, anger, and defensiveness. Validation of her feelings energized her to make changes in her self-care and create healthier boundaries with others.

Bruce had hidden his double life for a very long time. He harbored much shame for his one-night stands and was doubtful that respect from others, much less from himself, could be regained. Talking openly about feelings was uncomfortable, but he pushed himself to be more curious and self-reflective about his internal dialogue and the affairs. Accepting his flaws and his strengths energized the navel gazing work needed to repair his relationship.

William's shame from the years of engaging in online porn sites fed his critical self-talk. In therapy, he received unconditional respect, empathy, and validation and felt safe to unburden his heart. He needed to tell his story, own his guilt, imperfections, and strengthen his resolve to be the person he wanted to regain self-love. With help, he could recognize the positive parts of himself that showed up with his family and work. With a softened self-view, he could see the possibility for change and repentance.

Express your vulnerability to yourself and others to strengthen intimate connections. Rebuild your self-esteem, your sense of worth, and your goodness through activities that reflect your honest desire to change. When you act with integrity, others will notice. *If your restitution steps are genuine, respect from others will follow.* After addressing the journal prompts, start Step Two: Discover Who You Are.

I'm challenging you to embrace the following call to action: "I don't know exactly why I chose to have an affair, but I'm going to spend time looking deeper at my wrongdoing. I commit to this navel-gazing process to strengthen my empathy for those I have hurt and for myself. I will say out loud to myself and at least one other person what I'm discovering. Now, and in the future, I will try my best to do what is right."

JOURNAL PROMPT
EMPATHY FOR YOURSELF

Reflect on your present energy, emotional state, and your hopefulness (or lack thereof).

_____

_____

_____

_____

What do you miss about your life before the affair?

_____

_____

_____

_____

What do you miss about your life during your affair?

_____

_____

_____

_____

Reflect on your affair and identify the parts of yourself you don't want to lose.

_____

_____

_____

_____

_____

Reflect on how your affair exposure is affecting your social world, your family, and friends. How do you feel about the change in your community?

_____

_____

_____

_____

_____

What fears do you have related to this repair journey?

_____

_____

_____

_____

_____

How can you show more self-compassion? What self-talk do you need to incorporate?

_____

_____

_____

_____

_____

What do you need, and from whom, to continue this navel-gazing work?

_____

_____

_____

_____

SAY IT OUT LOUD. SHARE YOUR THOUGHTS WITH A TRUSTED FRIEND OR MENTAL HEALTH PROFESSIONAL.

STEP TWO: DISCOVER WHO YOU ARE

REFLECTIONS ON AFFAIRS

You know the statistics. 45% – 50% of marriages end in divorce. Financial and work stress, inferior physical and emotional intimacy, child-rearing pressure, and caregiving of older relatives are stressors that impact relationship success. According to the American Association for Marriage and Family Therapy (January 2018), 15% of married women and 25% of married men have had extramarital affairs. Note that the statistics are about 20% higher when there is no intercourse in a secret, emotional relationship.

An affair is a secret relationship withheld from your significant other. This relationship could be with someone from work, from one's friendship group, church, or neighborhood, or a sex worker from a club, massage parlor, or online. The affair may be committed in-person or entirely over chat or text. The secrecy leads to deception, a breach of trust, and a separate life that detaches one emotionally and sometimes physically from others.

Most people desire reliability, consistency, and permanence in their primary relationship, and they also crave adventure, novelty, and excitement. It is challenging to get all of these needs met by one person. Motivation to go outside of one's primary relationship is varied:

- Some begin an affair in search of better sex.
- Some begin an affair to satisfy emotional needs such as affection, connection, intimacy, and fun.
- Some have an affair because they want a self-esteem boost.
- Some have an affair to escape from stress or boredom at home.

Prominent researchers and marital experts have made the following conclusions about affairs:

- Affairs can quickly end a marriage and other relationships.
- Affairs can occur in marriages and relationships that, before the infidelity, were quite good.
- Affairs are fueled by secrecy and threatened by exposure.
- Relationships can, with effort, survive affairs once they are exposed.

Carmen was the stay-at-home mom of a toddler. She felt isolated, bored, and disconnected from her identity.

Online chatting fulfilled her needs for connection, ego strokes, and emotional support. Initially, she didn't feel like she was hurting her partner. But as her attachment with her online friend deepened, detachment from her partner Elena grew.

Bruce was a businessman who frequently traveled where he experienced boredom and isolation when away from home. These feelings, coupled with a sense of anonymity, led him to engage in a series of one-night stands. In his mind, he minimized the impact of the sexual encounters on his committed relationship at home. But the secrets kept building until Carlos found evidence of Bruce's infidelity.

Tasha, who was in a 30-year marriage, decided that her spouse relationship wasn't enough. She and Eric had mastered the art of cohabitation. In other words, they functioned well in taking care of their home and family but had grown emotionally detached. Even though they didn't argue often, Tasha, over the years, had built up much resentment. Her husband stated that he had been clueless about his wife's unhappiness until she left him after connecting with an old high school friend.

William worked the night shift. He was physically tired, struggling with his new role as a dad and husband, and under severe stress due to financial debt. Visiting pay-for-relationship sites oddly calmed his anxieties in the short term. Still, it often left him feeling incredibly guilty about his dishonesty and the financial strain placed on his family. His porn-site addiction negatively impacted his self-esteem.

Tom developed a close relationship with his assistant at work. They spent a lot of time together sharing work-related experiences that lead to a year-long affair. For Tom, the romance was fun and sexually satisfying. Meanwhile, at home, he and Chloe argued incessantly, and he progressively spent more time at work to avoid the conflict.

All of the individuals described above struggled with telling their affair story. All had partially answered questions but had never described at length what happened, when it happened, how they felt and how they had lived with the secret. Not only had they not told anyone else about their betrayal, but they also neglected to acknowledge it themselves. All side-stepped the confession, consciously or unconsciously, to avoid the harsh self-reflection of being a cheater.

Telling your affair story wholly and honestly is imperative to reparation and the journey toward forgiveness. I am guessing you have not shared with anyone details about your secret relationship. The following prompts will push you to reflect on your betrayal. Write without editing and say it all. Fight denial and minimization. Meet with a good friend or a mental health professional to share your story. It is time to share openly and explore your actions.

I'm challenging you to embrace the following call to action: "I don't know exactly why I chose to have an affair, but I'm going to spend time looking deeper into my wrongdoing. I commit to this navel-gazing process to strengthen my empathy for those I have hurt and for myself. I will say out loud to myself and at least one other person what I'm discovering. Now and in the future, I will try my best to do what is right."

JOURNAL PROMPT
YOUR AFFAIR

How did your affair start? What was it about the
relationship that was so tempting?

_____

_____

_____

_____

Reflect on the positive and negative memories of the
affair.

_____

_____

_____

_____

At the time of your affair, what was happening in your
life at home and work?

_____

_____

_____

What personal needs did your affair satisfy?

_____

_____

_____

_____

Reflect on the wounded's awareness and feelings about
your infidelity.

_____

_____

_____

_____

When did you start noticing that your happiness in the
affair was lessening, or did it?

_____

_____

_____

_____

Why was it so hard to stop?

_____

_____

_____

_____

How was your secret relationship discovered?

_____

_____

_____

How fully have you disclosed information about your affair?

_____

_____

_____

_____

How did it end? Or did it?

_____

_____

_____

_____

What losses are you grieving related to the affair?

_____

_____

_____

_____

SAY IT OUT LOUD. SHARE YOUR THOUGHTS WITH A TRUSTED FRIEND OR MENTAL HEALTH PROFESSIONAL.

NAVEL GAZING

Multiple individuals who have betrayed their partner have walked through the door of my counseling office. Some have come willingly, and others have entered with doubt and hesitation. Typically, the cheater is resistant to looking at their betrayals. It is challenging and humbling to admit a transgression and openly face the person you hurt. *Many violators hold on to the unrealistic hope that the words, "I'm sorry, and I won't do it again," will erase the violation.* The root of a sincere apology comes from a self-discovery process of navel gazing. Sound simple? As humans, we make extraordinary efforts to avoid sitting with our introspections and reflecting deeply on our behaviors. It is less emotionally challenging to focus on work, activities, and others. Thus, impactful events in our lives often go unexamined. Now it is time to examine the significant event of your affair by elevating your thoughts and feelings from the deep dark hole in your head and heart and bring your sins to light.

I am assuming others repeatedly ask why you strayed, cheated, and lied. Without navel gazing, your deflective answer of "I don't know" is part of the shield that blocks confrontation with your sin. We, as humans, unconsciously and consciously avoid being honest about our mistakes. Ironically, most of us can look in the mirror and fail to see our true reflection. Self-exploration can unlock the door to find meaning in your betrayal and repair connections with your partner, family, and friends.

The first step of navel-gazing is to BE CURIOUS. Don't push away the persistent question of "Why, why did you cheat?" It is easy to claim that you were suffering from temporary insanity during your affair, which is partially true. You probably can't recall all of your intentions, actions, and choices. But it is crucial to take the time to sit with your affair story and remember more of your motives, feelings, and thoughts. You are guilty. You hurt your partner and others. You made bad choices, and you must take responsibility for them and try to answer the "why" of your affair.

Be curious – notice and feel all of your emotions and their effects on others. Work to accept both your rational and irrational feelings. We typically embrace our happiness and accomplishments but shut off and deny our sadness, anger, shame, and loneliness. This internal exploration is challenging, but avoiding your story will consume your self-view, self-worth, conscious and unconscious feelings, thoughts, and actions. You cannot erase the affair, but reflective clarity creates internal and relational change. Let me emphasize this – analyzing the past's unchangeable acts will generate a precise identity of the changes needed to be happier in the future.

Awareness is a call for action. Owning your "stuff" and humanness will free your spirits, hopes, faith, and joy. *Accept your imperfect self – a self who can make a change.* You are an individual of worth who is flawed, fallible, and hopefully humble in your desire to repair the damage inflicted on others. Acknowledging the pain and vulnerability is a sign of strength, not weakness. With in-depth exploration and acceptance of your feelings, thoughts, and actions, you will no longer fear their expression, and you will grow in your authenticity. Openness, humility, and the absence of your secret life will build your sense of worth and open the door for more intimate relationships.

I encourage you to look in the mirror with curiosity and with the hope of discovering your true self. *How did you get to a place where you quit acting in congruence with your values, beliefs, goals, and public image?* Did work, sex, porn, video games, alcohol, or your ego block you from acting with integrity? All the illustrated adulterers admitted that they struggled with the incongruence of their true self and their betrayal. Embarrassment, guilt, and shame surfaced with the truth-telling of their affair.

- Bruce confessed that alcohol played a significant role in his serial affairs. His over-indulgence led him to be more impulsive and to abandon his self-control. His behavior on business trips did not reflect the man who was an attentive partner and friend at home.

- Tom's successful work identity and ego kept him from prioritizing his relationships at home. He found that his identity as a pillar of his church and community became tainted once others learned of his affair. He resisted accepting that others now perceived him negatively.

- Elena, who was typically open and honest, was detached from her true self by embracing secretiveness and deception and minimized her online relationship's intensity. She violated her values and commitment to her wife.

- Tasha's identity as a selfless helper of others was incongruent with her selfish justification of her affair. She denied responsibility for the pain caused by her relationship outside of her marriage with her spouse and family.

- William's addiction to porn intensified as his stress level rose with the responsibilities of home and work. His diminished self-worth masked the fact that he was a very hard worker, responsible, and committed to his job and family.

It is typical to look at yourself in black and white terms: good or bad; honest or a liar. But humans are too complex to be lumped into an either/or category. Ironically one can be rule-following and rebellious, generous, and selfish, open, and secretive. Your goal is to admit your sins without completely condemning yourself and falling deep into despair and inaction. Accept that you are human, full of good character qualities, and imperfect. Look hard into the mirror and integrate the person you were before the affair with the person you are today and the person you want to be in the future. You are the total of all that has happened and all that will happen. As a human, you are continually changing. Repair comes from identifying how you want to be different and then committing to that change. Your deepest struggles may reveal your most profound strengths. Reconnect and re-discover your strengths of persistence, humility, flexibility, intentionality, generosity, devotion, honesty, reliability, and curiosity.

The feeling of guilt is an excellent sign that you are ready to face your betrayal, show remorse, and own your behavior. Accept that your infidelity has inflicted much pain on others. Be compassionate and empathetic to the wounded and family. Guilt is different from shame. Shame manifests when you carry the belief that you are an irreparably damaged person. Such feelings can only create greater separation between you and your significant other because they imply resignation – the antithesis of reparative change. *Guilt inspires action, repentance, and resolutions.*

Consider the powerful triad of your thoughts, feelings, and actions. You must understand how the three work together. We live in a "just do it" culture that often minimizes the power of our wants, desires, and emotions. Actions are strongly affected by your thoughts and feelings, and conversely, your thoughts impact your feelings. Accept the power of their interaction. If you wish to be different, it is essential to process your internal thoughts and feelings. The task of navel gazing is to talk about YOURSELF. Don't get stuck analyzing the person you had an affair with, your significant other, or other factors. It's easy to place blame outside of yourself. The goal is to analyze you – your thoughts, feelings, actions, motivations, and character.

William struggled with shame about his online porn habits and his dishonesty. Since he saw himself as flawed beyond repair, he had no hope of repairing his relationship with his wife. Depressed with his self-image, William struggled with motivation to work toward change. He felt stuck, hopeless, and internalized a lot of the blame. He also finger-pointed at factors outside of himself that contributed to his failure to take care of his family's emotional and physical needs. William blamed the overnight work schedule that left him exhausted, prohibited him from spending time with his family, and made it difficult for him to attend Sex Anonymous meetings. He blamed the power of technology that made pornography sites accessible and easy to keep his visits secret. All were valid excuses that contributed to his poor behaviors, but ultimately, he needed to commit to making a change within the reality of his life.

Tasha came into therapy feeling stubborn about navel gazing. Resenting her years of caretaking of others, she felt justified in her affair. Taking care of children, elderly parents, a home, and work left her with a loss of energy and neglect of her wants and desires. She struggled to be reflective, to be self-critical, and to accept that she had, unconsciously, embraced the martyr role. She resented taking care of everyone else and felt it was her time to be more self-indulged. The relationship with an old schoolmate was fun and felt good – at least temporarily. She blamed her husband Eric for the dissolution of their relationship and talked about how he was uninvolved and boring. Tasha felt neither guilt nor shame over her affair and held little remorse for breaking of her marriage's covenant.

Tom blamed his wife, Chloe, for creating distance in their marriage. He voiced frustration that she spent too much time focused on the children, leaving little attention and energy for him. Tom claimed that her absence drove him to seek intimacy elsewhere. Since he had weak self-reflection skills, it was hard for him to analyze and embrace his thoughts, feelings, and actions. His defensive, robust ego shaded any feelings of guilt or shame. The navel-gazing work encouraged Tom to examine his resentments and say out loud his thoughts and feelings to enhance his self-understanding and build empathy for those he hurt.

Carmen initially wanted to place the blame on her internet friend, claiming that she was the one that first crossed the line into intimacy. While that may have been true, it was important for Carmen to own her actions that also fueled the secret relationship. Taking responsibility for the choice to have an intimate relationship only came after she navel gazed and reflected on her thoughts and feelings. She was lonely, emotionally detached from Elena, and resented the loss of her career.

Through navel gazing, Bruce realized that he was telling himself that his secret one-night stands weren't hurting anyone. He accepted that part of his faulty thinking also included self-justification. His self-talk included messages like, "I deserve a little fun since I have worked so hard. If I cheat away from home, I won't face temptation when I am back with Carlos." He challenged his attitude toward committed relationships and adjusted his behaviors. Once he forced himself to be more introspective, he connected with his embarrassment, sadness, and regret for hurting his partner.

Both Carmen and Bruce accepted responsibility for their betrayal and admitted their choices caused pain and hurt in their respective partners. They felt guilty and were determined to take steps to repair their relationships and to make a change. They were able to communicate remorse and empathy. Even though the road to redemption wasn't easy, they both found the energy to work to regain trust.

JOURNALING

Meanwhile, life goes on – pressures at work, responsibilities at home with your children, and extended family continue. It will be challenging to keep the spotlight on this process of navel gazing. It is much easier to take care of other things – car maintenance, laundry, or a work project since all of these activities hold little emotion from the exposure of your vulnerabilities. Acknowledge your responsibilities and have compassion for yourself while setting some routine for doing this introspective work for at least the next four to six weeks. Put a reminder in your phone to work on the next chapter every three to four days. Regular journaling will increase your mindfulness and keep you focused on the repair work. The guided journal prompts in *More Than Sorry* will pace your work and lead you to deeper self-connection. Unlike a diary, which is more of a report of events, journaling asks for internal revelation and processing. Reading your work aloud will also help you hear yourself and provide more clarity and ownership of your thoughts and feelings. Check-in and simply ask yourself, "How am I doing?" "What do I want?" and "What do I need?" You will be surprised what ah-ha's occurs once you sit quietly with yourself.

Write without editing. Purchase a journal of your liking or set up a password-protected file on your computer. Make sure you explain to your partner that this work mandates that you take the time to explore yourself without fear of others reading it. Ask them to respect your privacy. Reassure others that you will, at some future point, share more of your inner world. Also, consider talking to someone you trust, like a mental health professional or a close friend, to share your journaling experience. This reflective process ultimately leads you to the journal prompt, Ask for Forgiveness, in which you write an honest, open, and sincere apology letter to those you hurt.

Commit to the process of guided journaling and reap the rewards. The benefits are many. Through navel gazing, you will build your self-love and respect, strengthen your values, and work toward forgiving yourself. You will improve your self-reliance and confidence. Trust that what you have to say is significant. Honor yourself with time for reflection. As you look back you are also processing what is happening now and what you dream for in the future. Finding clarity for your hopes will shape your motivations and, ultimately, your life priorities and goals.

As you work through the prompts, you will explore

your thoughts, feelings, desires, and goals. Moving through this process can be emotionally intense and overwhelming. You may uncover repressed memories of your affair and the pain you have inflicted on others. *Recognize that the more honest you are with yourself, the more open you will be with others.* Through deeper self-awareness, your self-compassion will build, as will your empathy for others.

Journaling will help you learn more about yourself – who you were in the past, in the present, and who you hope to be in the future. In finding the written words to describe your experiences, you will, in turn, be able to articulate more clearly to others what you are processing and discovering. *You are learning to "say out loud" what you are thinking and feeling – an essential skill for building intimacy.*

Occasionally re-read your work and notice your growth. Since this work is emotionally challenging, treat yourself as you would treat someone you love – with patience and compassion. Accept your humanness as one who is not perfect but who can make a change. Take an observer's view of your navel-gazing journey. Don't let yourself get stuck in self-pity but work to self-analyze and plan for changes in your present and future relationships.

While this process may expose your regret, pain, shame, and guilt, I also believe that journaling will clear space for hope – hope for repaired relationships with others and with yourself. Fear may be holding you back – fear of exposing your secrets. Since journaling should be private and confidential, what do you have to lose? *What negative effects could come from honestly sharing your betrayal story?* Your affair story is mixed with pain and joy and reflects your imperfection and goals for change. Your inner strength comes from having the courage to look inward and own your thoughts, feelings, and actions.

PRACTICE MINDFULNESS

Along with the guided journal prompts, I encourage you to sit with yourself daily and allow the quiet to send you guiding messages. Practice mindfulness by setting an intention to be more aware of your thoughts, feelings, and physical sensations. Slow down and pay attention without judgment to what you are experiencing. Accept and notice your internal processes without trying to interpret them. Take the time to stop and focus on the now. Staying in the present will lead to your self-acceptance and clarify the goals you wish to set.

Mindfulness is the opposite of busyness. Just breathe – in and out slowly. Pay attention to the rise and fall of your chest as the oxygen flows in and out. Do this several times a day. The practice of mindfulness will calm you, relieve stress, improve your sleep, and gastrointestinal issues.

Search the app store on your phone, and you will find meditation aides available – many that are free. When is the best time for quiet reflection? Mornings may give you some direction for your day, whereas evenings may facilitate deeper examinations. Can you take 10–15 minutes in the morning, during your lunch break, or before bed to sit in stillness?

The goal is to be authentic in 'walking your talk.' I apologize for the cliché, but it is crucial to own your sins to lead a life filled with integrity where your actions are congruent with your beliefs and words. Take this opportunity to move in a different direction. I am asking you to trust the process of this guided navel gazing. It is time to start.

———

I'm challenging you to embrace the following call to action: "I don't know exactly why I chose to have an affair, but I'm going to spend time looking deeper into my wrongdoing. I commit to this navel-gazing process to strengthen my empathy for those I have hurt and for myself. I will say out loud to myself and at least one other person what I'm discovering. Now and in the future, I will try my best to do what is right."

JOURNAL PROMPT
NAVEL GAZING

Today, how would you answer the question of WHY?
Why did you have an affair? Guess your motivation.

_____

_____

_____

_____

_____

What were you feeling and thinking then about yourself
and your primary relationship? What are you feeling and
thinking now?

_____

_____

_____

_____

_____

Acknowledge the guilt of your actions. How did you hurt others?

_____

_____

_____

_____

With humility, reflect on your human flaws.

_____

_____

_____

_____

Reflect on the loss of your authentic self. Did your actions match who you are?

_____

_____

_____

_____

List your strengths that will lead to relationship repair.

_____

_____

_____

_____

SAY IT OUT LOUD. SHARE YOUR THOUGHTS WITH A
TRUSTED FRIEND OR MENTAL HEALTH PROFESSIONAL.

THE BRAIN AND SEX

D id it feel like you lost your common sense during your affair? There is much research on how powerfully sex and falling in love affect the human brain. The logical reasoning part, called the lateral orbitofrontal cortex, is responsible for reason, decision-making, and value judgments. This part of the brain shuts down during sex, resulting in less inhibition and increased impulsivity and boldness. In other words, the intensity of sex and lust can be beautiful, dangerous, and destructive.

Continuing with this mini-teach on brain science, understand that in the context of an affair, the brain stirs up dopamine, serotonin, oxytocin, prolactin, and testosterone. These hormones contribute to impulsivity, poor decision-making, and intense energy, emotions, and feelings of possessiveness. There are also positive effects from this cocktail on one's physical health and mood.

I once had a client who justified his extramarital affair by saying with a big smile on his face, "It feels so good it has to be true love - it has to be right." On the contrary, the dopamine flood in his brain from the secret relationship had distorted his rational thinking. Hormones, combined with heightened emotions, block cold logic. He struggled to accept that his feelings were more potent than his ability to reason. Lust obscured his ability to see the consequences of his actions.

Moreover, having an orgasm stimulates the brain in the same way as drugs, listening to music, eating a favorite food, winning at sports, and gambling. The brain does not differentiate much between these activities and sex. Scientists have observed brain scans that illustrate how the brain lights up in the same way when engaged in these activities.

Affairs can be addictive, just like sex, substance abuse, gambling, and overeating. The brain registers the pleasure in these activities, and cravings begin. Your logical mind, the part that shuts down when you actively engage in an affair, doesn't communicate the dangers and negative consequences you will experience. After feeling pure euphoria, your brain receives the message to come back for more. William, who had a long-time relationship with porn sites, and Steve, who had numerous one-night stands, experienced the physiological and emotional outcomes described. Both men used sex to relieve stress and isolation and to achieve a sense of calm.

Similar symptoms of alcohol and sex addiction are:

- Increased craving or obsessive desire for more
- Loss of interest in activities

- Mood changes – more irritability and resentment
- Loss of moral code
- Failed attempts to stop
- Secrecy and lying to cover behaviors
- Feelings of guilt and remorse
- Financial or work-related consequences

Professionals describe the state of the brain during an affair and falling in love as being in a state of temporary insanity. It is common to regress to an adolescent need for adventure, regardless of consequences, when stimulated by illicit sex. Lust is a kind of madness – a madness that rarely lasts. Passion takes a lot of metabolic energy to maintain and eventually slips away. Tom's relationship with his co-worker lost energetic power over time, especially when they both started experiencing the negative consequences of their relationship. The neurochemical high from their affair diminished with increased struggles at home and heightened danger of losing their jobs since their romance violated company policy.

I share this information about brain chemistry not to forgive and rationalize your poor decisions and dishonesty. I suspect you were semi-conscious of the consequences of your secrets. You knew you had crossed the line in your commitments, and, despite your rush of hormones, you still had the power to STOP and walk away from the dark choices. Once the energy from lust clears, slow down and listen to your inner knowing. Trust that clarity will come once your brain calms down.

Neurologists have identified this as neuroplasticity. The brain changes with each experience and with knowledge. Continue the path spelled out in *More Than Sorry*, enhancing your self-knowledge to avoid repetition of past mistakes.

I'm challenging you to embrace the following call to action: "I don't know exactly why I chose to have an affair, but I'm going to spend time looking deeper into my wrongdoing. I commit to this navel-gazing process to strengthen my empathy for those I have hurt and for myself. I will say out loud to myself and at least one other person what I'm discovering. Now and in the future, I will try my best to do what is right."

JOURNAL PROMPT
YOUR BRAIN

How does the phrase "temporary insanity" resonate with your reflections of your affair?

_____

_____

_____

_____

_____

Does the information on brain chemistry feel relevant to your affair experience? How?

_____

_____

_____

_____

_____

Reflect on your feelings for the other during the affair.
Remember your obsessions, thoughts, range of moods,
and your guilt.

_____

_____

_____

_____

_____

How much did you think about the wounded during the
affair? How did your feelings change toward your partner
change?

_____

_____

_____

_____

_____

Assuming you made bad decisions during the affair, what
were some of the worst ones?

_____

_____

_____

_____

_____

SAY IT OUT LOUD. SHARE YOUR THOUGHTS WITH A
TRUSTED FRIEND OR MENTAL HEALTH PROFESSIONAL.

TAKE A MORAL INVENTORY

The Golden Rule asks you to treat others as you want them to treat you. Your affair harmed people you cared for, and you violated a universal moral code. The temptation was fueled by your low moral commitment, by its secrecy, and cemented in the fact that you were temporarily successful in your deception. Lying is addictive. The more falsehoods you told led to the telling of more lies.

During the affair, was your intuition – that little voice in your head – trying to remind you that you were hurting others and making bad choices that violated commitments and expectations? You didn't stop and listen to your internal knowing of right versus wrong. Examining your loss of values may feel like scraping your fingers across a blackboard. It is uncomfortable to confess wrongdoings, and you will unconsciously work to avoid being honest with yourself and others. Being forthright takes courage. Repent and own the pain your secrets have caused to reconnect with the parts of you that deserve love and respect.

Let's face it, getting caught and having your secrets exposed was a huge motivation to look honestly in the mirror and face the consequences of your betrayal. Once others discovered your secret relationship, did you start to feel differently about yourself and your choices? Once caught, you probably grasped how others saw you. How did you react upon your betrayal's exposure? I am guessing that initially, you pushed back and denied your actions. I assume embarrassment, guilt, and shame followed.

Why did you lie when initially confronted? Pause for a minute and ponder this question. What answer first popped into your head? Write it down and analyze your reason. Perhaps you wanted to protect your image with family and friends. Perhaps you tried to shield the other from being exposed while preserving the fun of the secret relationship. Were you aware that your affair violated a moral code and your value system?

If you can't self-observe, then you can't self-correct. Engage your curiosity and self-analytical skills – question how you went down the road to living a secret life. Be curious about how you justified, in your mind, dishonesty. We have already discussed the affair-brain that blurred your logical reasoning. Before the affair, were you more honest, trustworthy, respectful, responsible, and loyal? How would you have described your character then? Was there previously a pattern of bad choices that negatively impacted relationships, career paths, or legal concerns?

Can you identify beliefs that influenced you to violate

your moral code? *What are the conscious and unconscious attitudes you hold about entitlement, commitment, honesty, loyalty, monogamy, and extramarital sex?* Evaluate the statements below.

- It is okay to cheat on your partner if they don't find out.
- What your partner doesn't know about cheating won't hurt them.
- Everyone cheats at some point in their relationship.
- Monogamy is an unnatural state.
- I wouldn't care if my partner cheated on me.
- Talking/flirting with someone is not cheating.
- Spending time on porn sites is not cheating.
- I am not an immoral person if I cheat.
- God will forgive me for cheating.
- Everyone deserves a little fun.

Tom was a good "family man." He attended his children's school activities, coached some of their sports teams, attended church regularly, and pitched in at home with chores. He was financially generous to many causes. He was successful at work and had achieved much respect as a leader and a forward thinker in his business. His justification of his double life was shattered once others discovered his affair. He looked in the mirror and grasped his betrayal that challenged his good-guy image. He struggled to reconcile who he believed he was with the person others saw. Tom then saw a diminished reflection of himself through the eyes of others.

Carmen admitted that she had frequently pushed the line in relationships. She flirted with others and was defensive as to the harm in "being friendly." She justified her online social media relationships as innocent since there was no physical contact. But it was a secret life, and it created an emotional distance in her marriage to Elena.

Bruce's history of one-night stands reflected his attitudes about monogamy and honesty. In his mind, he justified that one-night sexual encounters were not in violation of the covenant he made to Carlos. He thought that his secret life away from home did not violate their commitment to each other. After putting himself in Carlos's shoes, Bruce was able to accept that the discovery of the on-going betrayals had scarred Carlos and their relationship. Ironically, the discovery also scarred Bruce's self-image, and he accepted and challenged his dark side to work toward the repair.

These individuals had lost their integrity, a Latin word that means "whole." They no longer had an undivided life that came from qualities such as honesty and consistency of character. Wholeness demands integration of your public, private, and secret lives. Your divided life leads to a loss of your self-image as a genuine, open, and honest person. Thankfully, you can work to make meaningful changes. The person you were can be different from who you are now and who you will be in the future. You can move from self-centeredness to a more empathetic place. Your secret life can dissolve, and you can live with more integrity, more honesty, and openness. Your external actions can match who you are internally. You can evolve and become one who does no harm to others and treats others with respect. *Just imagine the inner peace you will gain from living a more honest, open life.*

————————

I'm challenging you to embrace the following call to action: "I don't know exactly why I chose to have an affair, but I'm going to spend time looking deeper into my wrongdoing. I commit to this navel-gazing process to strengthen my empathy for those I have hurt and for myself. I will say out loud to myself and at least one other person what I'm discovering. Now and in the future, I will try my best to do what is right."

CHARACTER DEFECTS CHECKLIST

Identifying character defects helps you to be aware of potential weaknesses and prevents your return to sinful behavior. Check your identifying characteristics. Think about the ones that contributed to your poor decision-making.

_____ Addictive	_____ Hopeless	_____ Risk-Seeking
_____ Aggressive	_____ Immature	_____ Sarcastic
_____ Angry	_____ Impatient	_____ Self-Condemning
_____ Arrogant	_____ Indifferent	_____ Selfish
_____ Complainer	_____ Insight (lack of)	_____ Self-Justifying
_____ Critical of Others	_____ Intellectualized	_____ Self-Pitying
_____ Defensive	_____ Judgmental	_____ Shame (full of)
_____ Defiant	_____ Lazy	_____ Stubborn
_____ Depressive	_____ Loner	_____ Suspicious
_____ Dishonest	_____ Dependent	_____ Threatening
_____ Easily Bored	_____ Manipulative	_____ Victim Mentality
_____ Easily Distracted	_____ Martyr	_____ Vulgar
_____ Egocentric/Self-centered	_____ Minimize	_____ Lack of Empathy
_____ Entitled Attitude	_____ Mistrustful	_____ Resentful
_____ Envious	_____ Morally Weak	_____ Gullible
_____ Fatalistic Attitude	_____ Passive	_____ Gossipy
_____ Pessimistic	_____ Guarded Emotionally	_____ Perfectionist
_____ Fearful	_____ People Pleaser	_____ Rejecting
_____ Frustrate Easily	_____ Difficulty with Intimacy	

JOURNAL PROMPT
YOUR MORAL CODE

Do you see yourself as an adulterer? How does that feel?

_____

_____

_____

_____

At the time of the affair, did you see your romance as a violation of your moral code?

_____

_____

_____

_____

To answer, "why, did I lie?", analyze feelings of self-entitlement and/or justifications you made for the affair?

_____

_____

_____

_____

What attitudes did you hold regarding monogamy, commitment, and honesty?

_____

_____

_____

_____

What character flaws do you recognize in yourself? List your intentions for change in your moral code.

_____

_____

_____

_____

Who did you harm? How can you treat others more respectfully?

_____

_____

_____

_____

SAY IT OUT LOUD. SHARE YOUR THOUGHTS WITH A TRUSTED FRIEND OR MENTAL HEALTH PROFESSIONAL.

EXAMINE YOUR PERSONALITY STYLE

Without sending you too far down the rabbit hole of self-discovery, there are several personality inventories worth exploring. I do encourage you to pick one or more to examine. Often, these inventories validate what you already know about yourself. Your personality is your unique pattern of thinking, feeling, and behaving. *There is no perfect or preferred personality style, and there is no one style that is more inclined to have an affair.* These inventories are additional tools that will help you deepen your naval gazing. Better awareness of how you operate internally and interact with others will help in this self-analysis process.

The five dimensions of personality are often called the Big Five. Rate yourself on a spectrum of mild, moderate, and extreme. Recognize that your character can shift over time due to life experiences and maturity while your natural tendencies may be biologically ingrained.

1. Extravert (outgoing/energetic) vs. introvert (solitary/reserved): Do you get energy from being around people, or is it draining to be in a crowd? Do you prefer social situations or need alone time? Are you outward or inward turning?

2. Agreeableness (friendly/compassionate) vs. challenging/detached: People high in this trait are more empathetic and cooperative, while those low in this area are more competitive, disinterested in others, and tend to be more manipulative.

3. Openness (inventive/curious) vs. consistent/cautious: People high in openness have a broad range of interests and are eager to experience new things. They are risk-takers. Those low in this area don't like change and need consistency in their routines.

4. Conscientiousness (efficient/organized) vs. easy-going/careless: Responsible, goal-directed people are detail-oriented and productive. Those low in this area dislike schedules and have difficulty finishing projects. They are good procrastinators.

5. Neuroticism (sensitive/nervous) vs. secure/confident: Those who fall high on this trait are often anxious, irritable, riddled with self-doubt, and struggle with emotional stability. These individuals are complainers and dependent on others. Confident people

have a higher value of self-worth and self-competence.

In psychology, four domains of personality are identified. Most likely, you have abilities in all four areas, but it's interesting to determine which areas are most dominant.

1. Executing: achiever, responsible, deliberate, consistent
2. Influencing: communicator, self-assured
3. Relationship building: empathetic, harmonious, inclusive
4. Strategic thinking: analytical, strategic, intellectual, planner

If you take the Myers/Briggs Inventory or the 16PF personalized profiles, either will illustrate where you fall on the following indicators:

1. Extrovert vs. introvert (an attitude)
2. Sensation vs. intuition (how you gather information)
3. Thinking vs. feeling (reflects how you make decisions)
4. Judging vs. perceiving (how you implement or apply knowledge to your world)

I recommend that you explore this topic through one of the following links:

- Typical Enneagram personality types by the Global Leadership Foundation: https://globalleadershipfoundation.com/deepening-understanding/enneagram/
- Manish Hatwaine's excellent review of 16 Personality Factor, The Big Five, the Keirsey Temperament Sorter, and the Myers-Briggs: https://myzenpath.com/self-discovery/personality-inventories/

It's tempting to diagnose our five couple's personalities and put them concretely into categories, but realistically, this is not possible. There are many aspects of one's character, and the description here of these individuals is limited. But we will put on our analyst hat and make some guesses to conceptualize the betrayers' strengths and weaknesses.

According to the inventories suggested here, we can guess:

- Carmen is "The Helper" because she is warm-hearted and a people pleaser who has difficulty acknowledging her own needs. She is an extrovert and scores high on optimism and appetite for socializing.
- Bruce is "The Achiever" who is highly accomplished, confident, and charming, but who is also somewhat self-conscious of his image. He struggles with workaholism but is generally cool-headed and an extrovert.
- William is "The Individualistic" who is

sensitive, reserved, moody, and self-conscious. He is an introvert, pervasively sad but conscientious.

- Tasha is "The Enthusiast" who is busy, extroverted, and over-extended. She is looking for new experiences and is a risk-taker but is often bad-tempered.
- Tom is "The Challenger" who is self-confident and aggressive. He has temper issues, is assertive and decisive, and resists showing vulnerability.

Remember that these individuals' personality traits fall on a spectrum that ranges from mild to severe and that their behavioral characteristics can change over time with focus, acceptance, and intentionality. I encourage you to self-reflect. Where do you fall on the range of personality characteristics?

I'm challenging you to embrace the following call to action: "I don't know exactly why I chose to have an affair, but I'm going to spend time looking deeper into my wrongdoing. I commit to this navel-gazing process to strengthen my empathy for those I have hurt and for myself. I will say out loud to myself and at least one other person what I'm discovering. Now and in the future, I will try my best to do what is right."

JOURNAL PROMPT
YOUR PERSONALITY STYLE

What did you learn about your personality style?
Describe yourself using the traits identified in the
personality inventories.

_____

_____

_____

_____

_____

What relationship challenges do you face when
considering your personality style?

_____

_____

_____

_____

_____

What personality traits possibly affected your choice to have an affair?

_____

_____

_____

_____

What personality traits do you want to work to change? How?

_____

_____

_____

_____

SAY IT OUT LOUD. SHARE YOUR THOUGHTS WITH A TRUSTED FRIEND OR MENTAL HEALTH PROFESSIONAL.

IDENTIFY YOUR DEFENSE MECHANISMS

Y ou may struggle with remembering parts of the affair. You may have consciously and unconsciously created dark holes in your memory. *To preserve one's self-esteem and positive self-view, humans have an innate ability to deny sins and flaws while minimizing the devastating impact of their poor choices and actions.* To move forward in your relationships with yourself and others positively, you must confront your defense mechanisms – the strategies you unconsciously engaged in to detach from your wrongdoings. Getting caught in your betrayal forces you to take responsibility for the lies. Remember how you processed and justified your affair in your mind? What did you say to yourself that blocked you from being honest and from facing the reality of your cheating? What did you say when confronted with your betrayal? I am guessing that you initially denied or minimized your actions.

Defense mechanisms safeguard the mind against feelings and thoughts that are too difficult for the conscious mind to handle and accept. They are a helpful tool in dealing with emotionally challenging losses and situations beyond your control, such as natural disasters or mistreatment from others. But defense mechanisms are also used to mask your dark side. For you to look in the mirror and see a cheater, a liar, and a selfish person is very difficult. Taking off the mask and being honest about your affair takes courage and willingness to sit with many uncomfortable feelings like guilt, shame, embarrassment, remorse, anger, and hurt. Our ego seeks ways to defend itself from looking at our actions that are unacceptable to our values. I am sure you are somewhat familiar with the defense mechanisms. I am illustrating eight that are frequently used by those who cheat.

1. *Denial* refutes that the affair happened. In hopes of not getting exposed or caught, the offender will lie to themselves and others about the violation. Denial can also lead the cheater to refute that their partner is at risk for sexually transmitted diseases, financial problems, and emotional trauma.

2. *Repression* is the unconscious blocking of unacceptable or stressful thoughts and feelings. Intense memories are often blocked if they are too painful or don't match one's self-view. Those who have affairs frequently say, "I don't remember," when asked for details of their offenses and stuff the memories into the recesses of the mind.

3. *Rationalizing* is when a different explanation

twists the reality of the offense. "Lots of people have flings. It's no big deal." "I got my seven-year itch taken care of. Now I will be more committed in our relationship." "I think my affair helped me be a better partner." "My affair didn't mean anything to me. I was not in love with the other. I just needed a stress release." "You were so angry all of the time. I felt like you wanted me to prove I was an idiot." Hear the illogical reasoning that attempts to justify the cheating?

4. *Minimizing* is the attempt to make the sin smaller – to deflate its significance. "She/He didn't mean that much to me." "I never had sex with him/her, so it wasn't cheating." "I only cheated when I was out of town, and it didn't take me away from the family." Notice how the minimizer doesn't take responsibility for the magnitude of their affair on others.

5. *Theorizing* is an attempt to pull the discussion toward abstract, generalized theories around cheating to take the focus off of their wrongdoing. Internal self-talk and engaging others in discussion of hypotheses around affairs defend the cheater from looking at their misconduct. "Did you know that monogamy is an unnatural state?" "Most in the animal kingdom doesn't stick with one partner." "Many Europeans have open relationships." "All people cheat at one time or

another." There is no relationship where
everyone is candid all of the time."

6. *Regression* is when one is confronted with their
   sin and has childlike reactions. One might
   exhibit frequent temper tantrums with yelling,
   hitting, or crying. "You think you never
   messed up? Well, I'm sick of living with a
   saint! I hate you!" Those who regress may also
   act helpless. "I can't do anything right! I
   give up!"

7. *Justifying* is when the cheater finds a reason to
   explain their wrongdoing to feel better about
   their affair. "I cheated, and you spent a lot of
   money on clothes – we both had secrets!" "If
   you hadn't gone out of town so much, I
   wouldn't have been so lonely and would not
   have cheated." "Remember that fight we had,
   and you locked me out of the house? Well, I
   went looking for a way to get back at you."

8. *Compensation* is when one works hard in other
   areas to boost one's self-esteem and self-image
   by doing things that will garnish praise or
   internalized self-worth. During your affair, did
   you do more chores and projects at home? Did
   you spend more time with the kids? Did your
   volunteer work increase?

All of the naval-gazing individuals illustrated here
had engaged multiple defense mechanisms to cover their
betrayal, protect their egos, and strengthen their self-
esteem. All were guilty of denial – denying that the

choice to have an outside relationship violated the covenant made with their significant other.

- Carmen minimized her social media relationships.
- Bruce rationalized that his out-of-town affairs didn't affect his real life at home and used humor to deflect the tough talk.
- Tasha used compensation by being a super caregiver to her elderly parents and a community volunteer.
- William repressed memories of his long-time use of porn to escape the stress from everyday life.
- Tom regressed into angry rages and stonewalling when confronted with his cheating.

Strangely, our defense mechanisms make it possible to get more comfortable living in the lie rather than to risk exposure. Yet the work to cover up an affair takes a toll on one's peace of mind and physical and emotional health. Living with the anxiety of being exposed, coupled with shame, depletes one's energy. You were in the habit of not accepting your behaviors' truth, and I'm guessing your body and mood suffered.

You now have the choice to challenge the unconscious and conscious motivations and to be more fully transparent. Without your protective defenses, you will show up in the world in a more authentic way. The bonus to being received more positively by others is that you too will like yourself more. The journey to peel away your protective masks is very challenging. Remember to have compassion for yourself as you examine your defense mechanisms.

———

I'm challenging you to embrace the following call to action: "I don't know exactly why I chose to have an affair, but I'm going to spend time looking deeper into my wrongdoing. I commit to this navel-gazing process to strengthen my empathy for those I have hurt and for myself. I will say out loud to myself and at least one other person what I'm discovering. Now and in the future, I will try my best to do what is right."

Defensive Mask Checklist

Attempts to Hide Your Wrongdoings

Denial	Repression	Rationalizing	Minimizing
Theorizing	Justifying	Regression	Compensation

Underlying Feelings

Sad   Lonely   Hurt   Inadequate   Fearful   Angry   Guilt   Shame

Defensive Masks

Being Perfect	Attacking	Being Sarcastic	Agreeing
Blaming Others	Being Critical	Judging Others	Joking
People Pleasing	Apologizing	Controlling	Being Silent
Self-Deprecating	Being Cold	Evading Questions	Denial
Avoiding Others	Busyness	Repression	Fantasizing

How I Think Others Perceive Me

Superior	Defiant	Indifferent	Manipulative
Immoral	Arrogant	Phony	Sullen
Super Straight	Angry	People Pleaser	Stubborn
Stressed	Depressed	Controlling	Aloof
Self-Pitying	Martyr	Manic	Passive

JOURNAL PROMPT
YOUR DEFENSE MECHANISMS

Denial: Did you deny the affair? Did you deny that your secret relationship could end your marriage and hurt your family? Did you lie and hope not to get caught?

_____

_____

_____

_____

_____

Minimizing: Did you refuse to acknowledge the moral and relational impact of your affair?

_____

_____

_____

_____

_____

Repression: Did you shut off memories of your actions?

_____

_____

_____

_____

_____

Regression: Did you throw temper-tantrums or exhibit other childlike behaviors during the affair and the discovery?

_____

_____

_____

_____

_____

Compensation: Did you work hard to look good in other areas of your life, such as parenting, work, or as a devoted church member?

_____

_____

_____

_____

_____

Rationalization: Did you intellectualize or try to explain away any of your unacceptable choices?

_____

_____

_____

<u>Theorizing</u>: Did you adopt a theory or hypothesis to explain your betrayal?

_____

_____

_____

_____

_____

<u>Justifying</u>: Did you point your finger at others to justify your betrayal?

_____

_____

_____

_____

_____

SAY IT OUT LOUD. SHARE YOUR THOUGHTS WITH A TRUSTED FRIEND OR MENTAL HEALTH PROFESSIONAL.

EXAMINE YOUR RELATIONSHIP STYLE

All humans need connection with other people. *Wired for attachment at birth, we learn how to connect with others over a lifetime.* Our relationship experiences with parents, friends, and early romances significantly impact our future attachments, self-esteem, confidence, and sense of worth. As you continue to read, reflect on any personal relationship patterns from your past.

There are three unique attachment styles: secure, anxious, and avoidant. But we, as humans, are way too complicated to be described in just a few sentences. The purpose of the information below is to stimulate self-analysis to help you make good guesses about who you are and why you chose to betray your significant other.

Securely attached individuals typically had healthy childhoods and have had more successful intimate relationships. A successful relationship is one where trust and mutual independence is balanced with dependence, commitment, intimacy, and support. In these healthy relationships, there is little game playing, defensiveness, and criticism. Conflict is handled successfully through empathy, listening, and a collaborative spirit. As beneficial as this sounds, having a secure attachment doesn't always protect one from having an affair.

Tasha likely falls into this category. She is secure in her attachment to her family and friends and even to her husband, Eric. Up until the time of her affair, she was committed to her marriage. They had few conflicts and were comfortable and content in their relationship, even though she admitted that she felt loved but not desired or wanted. Consequently, her healthy background did not stop her from straying. Tasha's outside relationship provided the thrill of a new relationship and stroked her ego. She resented taking care of others and didn't "say out loud" her feelings to get what she needed from her husband, family, and friends. In her affair, it was easier to attain intimacy with the other since she was more open, present, and vulnerable. Consequently, she felt more attached to her old high school flame.

Anxiously attached people struggle in relationships. Often, due to early trauma and weak parental bonding, there is a struggle with insecurity and fear of not being good enough – fear of abandonment results in co-dependent relationships. Often there are high expectations and reliance on a partner to rescue or complete them. To get more from a partner, anxious people often resort to game playing.

William seems to fit into this category. In the past, he had few relationships and often isolated himself with video games and porn sites where he could get emotional and physical thrills without risk of personal rejection. In all of his relationships, William had difficulty articulating his feelings and thoughts to achieve intimacy. He sent mixed signals. At times, he was supportive and present with his wife, and at other times, he self-isolated and detached from others. He felt inadequate in meeting the emotional, physical, and financial needs of his family. His insecurity resulted in moodiness and dependence on Kim to build his ego and carry the burden of taking care of the family. Ultimately, he held a lot of fear that his marriage would dissolve.

Carmen struggled with feeling safe and secure in her relationships. Her parents divorced when she was 10, and she had a fragile relationship with her dad. She was sexually assaulted at age 13 by a neighbor. She was hungry to be accepted and prioritized. She was confused about how to achieve intimacy. Before their child was born, the couple had excellent emotional and physical closeness. But, when faced with the challenges of being a stay-at-home mom, Carmen felt abandoned, bored, and lonely. Social media filled the void, and she intensely attached to her new friend while detaching from her partner, Elena.

The third relationship style is avoidant attachment. Due to early trauma and low parental connection, individuals in this category completely withdraw and avert relationships. This style protects them from being abandoned and hurt. With self-centeredness, they can emotionally distance themselves from their partners and exhibit intense mood swings.

Tom grew up with parents who told their children

never to show or discuss emotions. While being a star athlete and a good student, he was a rebellious teenager, drank heavily, and was sexually active. He masked feelings of fear, hurt, or worry with anger. Tom and Chloe successfully cohabitated, functioning well in the realm of family and household management, but they were not intimately or emotionally connected. They had volatile conflicts that were rarely resolved or repaired. Consequently, they frequently avoided each other and continued their pattern of cohabitation.

Bruce's sexual orientation was belittled and mocked during his teen years. He developed a strong sense of humor to cope with the conflicts. Although he dated a lot in his twenties, his first attached relationship was with Carlos. They described their relationship as relaxed, committed, and fun. All of this changed after the discovery of the one-night stands. Carlos communicated his pain, distrust, and hurt. Their discussions were difficult since Bruce could avoid and minimize the seriousness of their situation with humor. He is a funny guy but his humor blocked intimacy and repair. To reconcile, Bruce was challenged to be serious, authentic, honest, and share negative emotions such as fears, isolation, boredom, and worry.

By being aware of your attachment style, you can analyze how you achieve intimacy with your significant other and how you achieved intimacy with your affair partner. What intimacy differences do you acknowledge in your primary relationship and your affair relationship? Spend time reflecting on these polarities.

Also, you may see that there were parts of yourself in

your affair that you liked and regret their loss. With the other, notice differences in your energy, attitude, openness and risk-taking. Notice those aspects and reflect on how you can enhance those personal qualities in your current or future relationships.

———

I'm challenging you to embrace the following call to action: "I don't know exactly why I chose to have an affair, but I'm going to spend time looking deeper into my wrongdoing. I commit to this navel-gazing process to strengthen my empathy for those I have hurt and for myself. I will say out loud to myself and at least one other person what I'm discovering. Now, and in the future, I will try my best to do what is right."

JOURNAL PROMPT
YOUR RELATIONSHIP STYLE

1. Reflect on the level of intimacy you shared with your affair partner/the other.

- How open were you about your feelings and your thoughts?
- Were you a good listener? Were you curious about the other's life and challenges?
- How sexually intimate were you? Physically, did you ask for what you needed? Did you respond to what the other wanted?

_____

_____

_____

_____

_____

_____

2. How did you deal with conflict, control your anger, and problem-solve in your affair?

_____

_____

_____

_____

_____

_____

3. How much did you like the other? Were you positive or more critical? Did you communicate how much you wanted them? How so?

_____

_____

_____

_____

_____

_____

4. How much time did you spend planning activities that were fun, interesting, and intimate?

_____

_____

_____

_____

_____

5. What were the parts of yourself you liked while in the affair?

_____

_____

_____

_____

_____

6. What parts of yourself did you dislike while in the affair?

_____

_____

_____

_____

NEXT, ANSWER THE SAME SIX QUESTIONS REFLECTING ON YOUR RELATIONSHIP WITH THE WOUNDED.

What messages did you receive from your parents or other family members growing up that may have affected your choice to have an affair?

_____

_____

_____

_____

_____

How has your relationship with family and friends been affected by the exposure of your affair?

_____

_____

_____

_____

_____

_____

———————————

SAY IT OUT LOUD. SHARE YOUR THOUGHTS WITH A TRUSTED FRIEND OR MENTAL HEALTH PROFESSIONAL.

IDENTIFY YOUR COPING STRATEGIES

A sking for forgiveness, admitting your sin, and showing your vulnerability is hard! You are undoubtedly experiencing a roller coaster of emotions. At times, you may feel relief from shedding the burden of carrying the secret. In contrast, you may feel depressed, anxious, angry, defensive, embarrassed, fearful, and exhausted by the work of repair and the hyper-focus on your transgression.

During this intense period of repair, analyze your emotional barometer. Can you give yourself permission to identify and experience the wide range of your feelings? Can you regulate your emotions so that their expression doesn't inflict pain on you or others?

The stress of carrying a mental and emotional burden can affect one's cognitive, behavioral, relational, and physical health. There are multiple coping strategies that we engage in, both consciously and unconsciously, to handle intense emotions and future anxiety. Coping strategies can be positive and helpful or ineffective, self-sabotaging, and harmful. *Are your coping strategies helping you manage the painful emotions and allowing you to be present for the wounded and your family?*

Are you able to take care of yourself, physically and emotionally? Studies reflect that secret-keepers are more likely to have somatic issues such as headaches, nausea, and back pain. Are you engaged in any self-destructive behaviors such as substance abuse, online pornography, or gambling? Are you experiencing changes in your eating and sleeping? Are you crying more often? Are you experiencing intense anger more frequently?

I coach my clients to channel their inner parent during a crisis and instill a practice of self-care. Exercise and move – especially spend time outdoors, get restorative sleep, practice good nutrition (yes, avoiding processed food and other comfort food), minimize alcohol or other substance use, and find something to laugh about daily. The payoffs for healthy activities and exercise are sharper memory and thinking, higher self-esteem, better sleep, more energy, and stronger resilience.

Another coping strategy includes mindful breathing. When stressed, we unconsciously hold our breath. Focused breathing in and out of the nose for 15 minutes can help our attention, memory, and overall mental health. Find ways to step back when your emotions are tough to regulate and breathe, take a walk, or listen to music.

In addition to meditation and mindfulness, I want to add another practice that will shift your energy and attention in a positive direction. *Create a daily gratitude list.* This exercise may seem extremely difficult in light of all of the criticisms, the accusations, and the losses you are currently experiencing. The challenge is to look for and identify the positives in your life actively. Try to notice the birds singing, the smile from a passing stranger, or the fact that you and your partner can sit together around the dining table with family without tears or visible anger. Start a practice of writing down five things a day for which you are grateful. Notice how you feel – notice how a smile comes to your face and how your heart lightens when you focus on positives rather than dwelling on your struggles.

Unfortunately, Tom coped with the stress of his wife's discovery of his affair by working more. In addition to his long hours at the office that kept him away from home, he also used alcohol to sedate his feelings, which only fueled his isolation and anger. He did not take care of himself and ultimately became stuck in a pattern of anger and defensiveness.

Embarrassed by the online relationship's discovery, Carmen coped with the shame and conflict with excessive sleep and ice cream as a stress buster. Eventually, she got moving and joined an exercise community that helped her feel better physically and emotionally. Her energy increased, and her self-esteem improved through her connection with healthy, like-minded people. Her desire to repair her relationship with Elena heightened with her improved emotional state while her defensiveness dropped. Carmen shed shame. She was able to see herself in a more positive light and felt more trust and hope in repairing her relationship.

An important coping strategy is to confide in someone

who loves and likes you despite your wrongdoings. This trusted person cannot be the other or the wounded. It may be a mental health professional or a good friend. The act of being accountable, open, and honest to another will facilitate continued navel gazing. Initially, Tasha did not want to confide in her close friends. They noticed that she was avoiding them and was more distant. When she finally did open up to a trusted friend, the support encouraged her to dig deeper into her navel gazing. The frequent conversations helped her stay focused on natural, personal growth. She enhanced her senses of curiosity and compassion for herself and others.

As coached in the journal prompts, say it out loud. The reality is that sharing negative emotions won't exacerbate them. The fire tapers off once intense feelings are validated. Stuffed thoughts and feelings can lead to emotional explosions and self-destructive behaviors.

William attended Sex Addicts Anonymous groups. The 12-step program helped him keep an eye on his porn-site addiction and learn how to ask for help. Feeling comfortable at SAA meetings took some time. Learning how to be open and honest with fellow addicts was essential in being honest with himself and with Kim. To step up to the challenge of his night shift work hours, he and his wife worked together to establish systems at home to help him get at least six hours of sleep a day, which improved his mental and physical health.

Ironically, it is vital to incorporate some fun into your life and into your family life while doing the challenging work of navel-gazing. Positive experiences will help add vitality to your affair repair and provide needed breaks from the intense emotional work. Having fun positively affects one's overall mental health. Through laughter, endorphins release, and the stress hormone cortisol decreases, reducing anger and feelings of anxiety and sadness. What do you find fun? What makes you giggle? Is it a comedy show or dancing or music, trying new food, or spending time in nature? *Laughing and enjoying activities with your partner strengthens your connection and provides a foundation for moving forward with hope.*

Bruce, who had a great sense of humor, appropriately found ways to diffuse the intensity of his repair efforts with Carlos through silliness, fun, and play. With help from a therapist, he could also be serious, focused, and present when it was time for the tough talks. But it was the balance of play and seriousness that helped this couple deal with the transgressions while instilling much-needed levity.

Navel gazing and answering WHY is taxing work. Design a multi-faceted stress management plan inclusive of good sleep, nutrition, movement, and relational connection. Ask yourself what practices and routines help you stay grounded in the here and now. Consider your spiritual practice, whether it be a formal religious practice, meditation, service to others, or connection to nature. Accept the challenges of life and know that you are not alone in your failures. Breathe, pray, and stay curious and hopeful. While you know that you can't control everything, including how everyone will receive you, it is vital to hold on to hope for a happier, less stressful future. Implement healthy coping strategies to fuel this roller coaster ride. What looks like an ending may lead to a new beginning in your life.

I'm challenging you to embrace the following call to action: "I don't know exactly why I chose to have an affair, but I'm going to spend time looking deeper into my wrongdoing. I commit to this navel-gazing process to strengthen my empathy for those I have hurt and for myself. I will say out loud to myself and at least one other person what I'm discovering. Now and in the future, I will try my best to do what is right."

JOURNAL PROMPT
YOUR COPING MECHANISMS

Reflect on your current, positive self-care practices.

_____

_____

_____

_____

Evaluate your exercise, sleep, nutrition, meditation
and/or prayer, and time spent in nature.

_____

_____

_____

_____

_____

What stress reduction practices historically work for you?

_____

_____

_____

_____

Reflect on your emotional barometer. Do you know when you're feeling angry, scared, or sad? How well do you manage and express your emotions?

_____

_____

_____

_____

_____

What negative coping strategies do you need to change? Evaluate your use of alcohol or other drugs, eating habits, sleep patterns, amount of time spent watching television or playing video games, and social isolation.

_____

_____

_____

_____

_____

Reflect on your support community. Name two people, either a friend or a mental health professional, with whom you share your thoughts and feelings.

_____

_____

_____

_____

_____

List at least five fun activities you enjoy. Make sure your list includes things you can frequently do with a minimal financial burden. Make a plan to do a couple of these activities this week.

———————————————————————

———————————————————————

———————————————————————

———————————————————————

———————————————————————

———————————————————————

Start your gratitude list. What are five things for which you are grateful? Repeat this list daily.

———————————————————————

———————————————————————

———————————————————————

———————————————————————

———————————————————————

———————————————————————

———————

SAY IT OUT LOUD. SHARE YOUR THOUGHTS WITH A TRUSTED FRIEND OR MENTAL HEALTH PROFESSIONAL.

STEP THREE: SAY IT OUT LOUD

THE POWER OF SHARING

I n Step Two of *More Than Sorry*, you explored your morals, personality, defense mechanisms, relationship style, and coping mechanisms. Hopefully, you have deepened your insights into your affair through the process of self-discovery. At the end of each journal prompt, you have a directive to share your discoveries with a confidante. It is difficult to analyze your dark side alone. Step Three to deepen your apology for your infidelity, recognizes the power in saying it out loud.

Remember when your affair was first exposed? How did you feel when others learned of your secret life? You may have felt angry, scared, worried, and sickened that your secret was out. Maybe for the first time, the revelation of your double life forced you to realistically face the impact of your transgression as you witnessed others' view of your choice to cheat. *The public exposure of your affair changes everything.*

Your first inclination may be to isolate and do the navel gazing work singularly. You may feel you can handle this repair journey alone and cringe at the thought of exposing your inner world and wrongdoings with others. Freely sharing details of your affair may feel like self-flagellation but stuffing all your thoughts and feelings will lead to intense shame and self-hatred.

Exposing your dark side takes courage and humility as you face new expectations to be more open and honest. Tell the story of your affair and its recovery by writing freely in your journal and finding trusted confidantes with whom you can reflect openly about your experiences. It is normal to hide parts of your sin. It's normal to be worried about how others perceive you. But you must work through your resistance to completely share what happened, how you hid the secret relationship, and how you felt.

Saying it out loud to a trusted confidante will help you:

Feel supported in your repair journey.

You, as a human being, are worthy of love, respect, and second chances. Receive empathy for the challenges you face in this journey of seeking forgiveness. Sharing with a confidante will build your energy for this reflective and relational repair work and minimize discouragement. Having another accompany you on the walk to heal and grow will encourage your commitment to navel-gazing. Being accountable for the work to own your transgression is easier when supported by someone who cares for and motivates you without judgment.

Explore all your feelings in a safe place.

Sharing your infidelity with another will feel

uncomfortable and may feel risky. But if a safe place is available for you to be open, vulnerable, and honest, you will learn more about yourself, your guilt, and your humanness. Acknowledge your strengths and weaknesses by unburdening your heart with the revelation of your secrets. What is a safe place? It is where you feel respected and valued while being held accountable for your actions. Find a support person who minimizes their bias and judgment and protects your confidentiality.

With a mental health professional or a trusted friend, talk about feelings you don't want to express to the *wounded*. The revelation of your affair did not spontaneously stop your affections for the *other*, and it may not feel safe to say these emotions to your partner. Yet stuffing these feelings won't make them go away. Internalized, unacknowledged, and unexpressed emotions will only intensify. Permit yourself to process these feelings and figure out what to share with your significant other.

Facing the wounded's anger and hurt, over time, will deplete your energy to be present and continue working to meet your infidelity and deepen your apology. You may have mixed feelings for your partner that include sympathy, anger, resentment, and love. Yet, as the betrayer, you may not feel justified expressing negative emotions since you are the root of their extreme distress. Say out loud your fears, unhappiness, frustrations, and impatience in your journal and to a confidante to de-intensify your feelings, keep realistic expectations, and to accept the process of healing. Determine, with your supporter, what emotions to vent to the family or the wounded.

Reach clarity in self-understanding and setting of future intentions.

Saying out loud your inner thoughts and feelings to another, holds up a giant mirror that reflects your interior life, motivations, and actions. As discussed in the defense mechanisms section, you have probably minimized and rationalized your affair to some degree. Talking about it will shine the light on the reality of your transgressions. With this reflection, you will reach clarity to determine changes needed for relationship repair and growth. Learning to tune into your internal voice will help you strengthen your intuitive skills and recognize the aspects of yourself you hope to hold on to and which parts you want to change. You are giving voice to your wisdom by processing it with your confidante and clarifying redemption goals.

Experience the benefits of sharing your inner world.

As you *say out loud* your thoughts and feelings, you are allowing another to meet you at a vulnerable, deep place. The experience of trusting another to hear your inner thoughts hopefully models for you the benefits of being open. By letting someone else know you intimately, you receive validation, partnership, and a deeper connection. As a recipient of active listening, you experience its value and the power of empathy. Allowing others to see your vulnerable, open state will build the perception of you as authentic and trustworthy. You are no longer hiding behind a mask.

Hopefully, this positive experience will encourage you to be more open and empathetic with family and friends as you build deeper connections.

Who is the perfect confidante?

The paramount quality of a support person is that they are trustworthy, have skills in attentive listening, communicate empathy, and understand the importance of asking clarifying questions to help you see yourself more clearly. Mental health professionals, clergy, and other spiritual leaders trained to demonstrate unconditional respect will keep their biases at bay. Still, you may not have access, financially or geographically, to a professional. If this is the case, work to identify a friend or extended family member who naturally has the skills to be present, listen, clarify, and help you stay on the road to healing and growth. The perfect confidant is one you will turn to and take risks, show your vulnerability, and express your entire range of thoughts and feelings. It is difficult to honestly share transgressions with those who offer advice and pass judgment, but it is helpful to have your minimalizations and justifications confronted. Listen to feedback received and weigh the recommendations. Beware of complying with others' directives for the sole purpose of avoiding judgment and *you should* message. After processing with others, listen to your inner voice and act authentically with what you know are the proper steps.

A major struggle for most is how much detail and information to provide to the wounded and family. Yes, you are trying to be honest and more forthright. But the reality is, sharing lots of details specific to sex and locations won't help them heal. A vivid picture of you in the throes of passion will get stuck in their psyche and make it difficult for them to let go of the painful memories and look forward to a repaired relationship. But you can't stay silent. You must say out loud reassurance that you are processing your affair with your confidante to set restitution goals. Repeatedly acknowledge to the wounded that you made poor choices that hurt others and, through working with a confidante, you are learning more about yourself.

Tom resisted going to a mental health professional and did not want help repairing the marital damage from his affair. But Chloe drug him to couple's counseling, where he was reticent and silent. Consequently, the sessions yielded little progress since it became a platform for her to vent anger and mistrust while he said little to explain, defend or profess remorse. Eventually, Tom did confide in a friend who was able to listen, reflect, and encourage him to continue the process of navel-gazing. Within this relationship, Tom explored his thoughts, feelings, and desires. He expressed feelings for his affair partner and details of their secret relationship and processed resentments toward his wife. After venting these emotions, he was able to gain perspective and be more empathetic toward Chloe's hurt and anger.

Carmen reached out to supportive friends who helped her see the violation of her online relationship and listened as she expressed her sadness and grief in terminating the friendship with her internet friend. After saying out loud these feelings, she strengthened her resolve to sever her affair to repair her marriage and keep the family intact. She also received feedback on the importance of self-care. Friends encouraged joining social activities and professional outlets to re-engage in her music career. Receiving validation and empathy from her social network energized Carmen to prioritize her family while expanding ways to honor her own needs.

After processing her thoughts and feelings deeply with a therapist, Tasha came to understand that she had embraced a martyr stance that masked her genuine feelings of loneliness. She discovered that her stoicism and independent spirit had blocked the more profound connection with others. In therapy, she found a safe place to vent anger at her husband for the years of cohabitation. Most of her friends and family commiserated with Eric, who was the victim of her betrayal. For a time, her therapist was the only one with whom she could say aloud her criticisms and receive support and encouragement to continue to navel gaze. Although her friends were disappointed in her choice to have an extramarital affair, they did encourage her to look critically in the mirror at her violations. Tasha was able to make changes in her self-care and create healthier boundaries with others.

Bruce chose to seek professional help, finding a safe place to be open and confess his one-night stands. For the first time, he explored past traumas that deepened his insight and motivation to set goals for personal change. With newfound openness and deeper self-awareness, he could be more honest and show more vulnerability to Carlos and their friends. For the first time, intimacy in his connections was achieved emotionally without the entanglement with sexual encounters. Bruce was conflicted between a desire to be completely open with his partner while recognizing that the disclosure of details of his liaisons would severely enhance Carlos' level of anxiety and depression. With the help of the therapist, Bruce was able to practice ways to reassure his partner of his remorse and share his intentions for the repair of their relationship without divulging specific details of his multiple betrayals.

William was an introvert and struggled to be open and honest with others. He found a mental health therapist who provided a safe environment where he could shed the shame accumulated after years of engaging with pornography. It was only with feedback and support from a professional that the long process of healing could begin. He also gained the energy to say out loud his inner experiences with Kim. She was receptive and non-judgmental, which encouraged him to continue sharing his vulnerabilities, successes, and slips.

I will repeat – it is crucial to say it out loud to a therapist or trusted friend your repentant journey. It is a gift to receive validation and support from others. Through empathetic reflection of your thoughts and feelings, coupled with navel-gazing, you will regain self-love, self-acceptance, replenish your energy to change, deepen your apology, and work toward forgiveness. You are now ready to move on to Step Four and set your restitution goals.

I'm challenging you to embrace the following call to action: "I don't know exactly why I chose to have an affair, but I'm going to spend time looking deeper at my wrongdoing. I commit to this navel-gazing process to strengthen my empathy for those I have hurt and for myself. I will say out loud to myself and at least one other person what I'm discovering. Now, and in the future, I will try my best to do what is right."

JOURNAL PROMPT
THE EXPERIENCE OF SAYING IT OUT LOUD

Reflect on the moment your infidelity was exposed to your partner. How did you feel? How did you react?

_____

_____

_____

_____

Think about what you shared about your affair then and what has come out now.

_____

_____

_____

_____

Is it your nature to readily self-disclose?

_____

_____

_____

_____

What benefits have you found personally, and in your relationships, in being more open and revelatory of your inner world?

_____

_____

_____

_____

Reflect on your chosen confidante. What qualities do they have that make you feel safe to explore your affair?

_____

_____

_____

_____

_____

Have you been open and honest with your chosen confidante? Why or why not?

_____

_____

_____

_____

_____

How much have you said out loud to your partner about the details of your affair? How are you handling the questions?

_____

_____

_____

How much will you say out loud to family and friends about your affair?

_____

_____

_____

_____

_____

_____

———————

SAY IT OUT LOUD. SHARE YOUR THOUGHTS WITH A
TRUSTED FRIEND OR MENTAL HEALTH PROFESSIONAL.

STEP FOUR: SET RESTITUTION GOALS

REPAIR YOUR BROKEN RELATIONSHIPS

I t is difficult, after violating trust, to compensate for the injury you have inflicted on your significant other, your children, your extended family members, and your friends. The road to repair is long, challenging, and humbling. Continue to repeatedly apologize with sincerity and accept that there is no guarantee of a happy ending. *The words "I'm sorry" fall flat unless stated with genuine humbleness and remorse.* Communicate gratefulness for your family and friends' willingness to stay in your life despite your mistakes. Verbalize appreciation about being given a second chance. Here is a blueprint for Step Four to repair your relationships:

End the secret relationship.

Have you utterly committed to ending your secret relationship? Have you severed all contact with the other? Have you deleted their contact information on your devices and social media? The relationship with the other must be over, in all respects – entirely and forever. If you are still in contact, you can't do this work because you have continued to allow a third party's interference with your primary relationship and your family. Any connection with the other jeopardizes the hope of repair.

If you are still hanging on to contact with the other, process it with your confidantes. You must decide. Which relationship do you want? You may not feel completely clear in your desires. If that is the case, continue to navel gaze and deepen your self-understanding. I do recommend that you take a complete break from the other while you choose. Time and distance from the affair may provide clarity. Remember the chapter on the brain and sex? Regardless of your decision, it is time to pick and act accordingly. Recognize that leading a double life is not fair to all the involved parties. Put yourself in their shoes – have empathy.

Chloe wasn't confident that the affair had ended since Tom continued to have daily contact with the other at work. He did not openly share information about the dynamic of the working relationship. Consequently, the couple's repair, marred by mistrust and lack of openness, was stilted.

Initially, Tasha was not remorseful and was defensive about her outside relationship. Consequently, her family held a lot of hostility and resentment toward her. These relationships suffered even more because she didn't stop the exposed affair.

Initiate talk about your affair.

I am sure you are exhausted and irritated by the continual discussion of the betrayal. Note that reluctance to share your affair story and repair journey with the wounded and your family deepens their suspicions of more secrets held. I strongly suggest that you make a habit of checking in with them frequently. A simple "How are you?" reflects curiosity and focus on their healing, encourages openness, and intimacy.

The goal is to use the affair as an opportunity to have more in-depth conversations, connections, and intimacy than you ever had before. Building intimacy requires both partners to say out loud what they are feeling and thinking through gut-level sharing. Since trust at this point in your relationship is low, verbalizing thoughts and feelings may feel risky. The risk of rejection is real. But you must find the courage to share internal thoughts and feelings and to confess your failures and weaknesses. *When you share vulnerabilities and anxieties, intimacy is enhanced.* Listen to your partner with curiosity and empathy.

At first, Bruce resented having to rehash his repeated betrayals. But eventually, he realized that it was the "elephant in the living room" and that the best way to deal with it was to acknowledge it directly by continually and sincerely apologizing and showing remorse. He could sense when Carlos was upset. Instead of letting awkward silence continue, Bruce found the courage to check in and encourage his partner to talk about his thoughts and feelings.

. . .

Recognize when your significant other and family are triggered.

Events outside of your control, such as a public figure caught in a compromising relationship or a movie's plot involving someone having an affair, will impact the wounded. Periodically relapsing into the intense emotion triggered by the memory of your violation is normal. Random events, including places, people, and things, can prompt the flood of painful memories, feelings, and even somatic symptoms. Intuitively, you can sense when your significant other is emotionally revisiting the affair. Re-experiencing uncomfortable emotions are discouraging for them and you. Hopefully, with your courageous openness, the triggered emotions won't last as long and will happen less frequently in the future. Ask about their thoughts and feelings, reflect, validate, and listen. *And yes, say "I'm sorry" for the billionth time.*

Eric was triggered each time he drove by the high school where his wife had reconnected with her past friend. A trigger for both Chloe and Carlos was when their spouses weren't open and forthright about their work relationships. Kim and Elena had to deal with their discomfort when they saw their partner on their phone or computer.

Be an open book.

Be forthright about your social interactions and activities. Voluntarily offer reassurance that you are no longer hiding things. Yes, you may have to let go of previous interests linked to parts of your secret life. You will need to share your passwords, calendar, and bank statements with your partner, who will, undoubtedly, be checking up on you. You may resent making this sacrifice, but trust that the hyper-focus on you won't last forever. Humbly accept this relatively short loss of privacy. Process your resentment through your navel-gazing strategies. Trust will build if you continue to be open and self-revelatory.

Elena frequently monitored Carmen's online activities. At first, she resented the loss of privacy until she accepted that her wife needed the reassurance that trust boundaries were honored. Similarly, Kim tracked William's time on his computer. Attempts at hiding his porn site visits were typically unsuccessful. Eventually, William was more transparent and honest, knowing that his lies and secrets were adding to their marriage's brokenness. Carlos and Chloe asked their respective partners for access to their work-related phone records.

Be present and attentive.

Look at the specific interactions you and your affair partner had. Notice locations, activities, and gifts you shared and recognize how they may evoke emotional triggers for your partner. Driving by a hotel or restaurant, watching you on social media, or specific dates may cause your significant other to feel angry, hurt, sad, to ask more questions. The need for reassurance that the affair is over may intensify. Change your daily routine to include time to be present and fully participate in the lives of your partner and family. Be honest and accept that you were distracted and detached when you were hyper-focused on your secret relationship. The mere act of showing up demonstrates your intentions to be different. Active engagement in the lives of the wounded and your family communicates your determination to strengthen connections and make amends.

I recommend reading Gary Chapman's book, *The Five Love Languages*[1] , with your significant other. The quizzes will give insight into how you and your partner want to feel loved. The concrete tips will help you facilitate an action plan to show your partner love, compassion, and remorse. Through the quiz on www.5lovelanguages.com, you can prioritize your partner's needs for words of affection, physical touch, acts of service, gifts, or quality time. The challenge is to accept that the wounded's desires and needs may not match yours. Viva la difference!

Build intimacy.

The word "intimacy" suggests that passionate and romantic sex is the only way to connect on a deeper level. As you read on, you will see different types of intimacy that all center on the safe expression of mutual vulnerability in shared experiences. Let's look at different types of connections and recognize that the peculiarities of couples vary. Asking yourself the following questions will build your understanding of intimacy and inspire you to set other intentions in your relationships.

EMOTIONAL INTIMACY:
Mutually share your feelings openly.

- Do you talk about your internal experiences?
- Do you talk about how you feel about your partner and your relationship?
- Do you talk romantically with your partner?
- Do you give sincere compliments not only for what your partner does but for who your partner is as a person?
- Do you make sacrifices for your relationship?
- Does your partner feel loved and liked by you?

INTELLECTUAL INTIMACY:
Mutually discuss a variety of shared interests and ideas.

- Do you engage in discussions about current events, literature, or art?
- Do you share your work challenges?
- Are you interested in your partner's work life?

PHYSICAL INTIMACY:
Use touch and sex to feel connected.

- Do you touch each other frequently?
- Do you hold hands? Do you cuddle?
- Do you have rituals of hugs/kisses or of hello/goodbye?
- Do you have sex regularly?
- Are you sexually responsive?

EXPERIENTIAL INTIMACY:
Mutually share activities.

- Do you invest in quality time together?
- Do you engage in new activities together?
- Do you play together?
- Do you find ways to laugh together?

SPIRITUAL INTIMACY:
Mutually share beliefs about life's purpose, death, God, a higher power, or the power of nature.

- Do you share your meaning and purpose in life?
- Do you discuss your beliefs in a higher power or religion?
- Do you share your spiritual practices such as prayer, meditation, or connection with nature?

Tom and Chloe worked to show more interest in each other's work lives. While they struggled to share emotional intimacy, they worked on their friendship. They strove to learn more about each other individually and to be more active in their children's lives as a couple.

Elena and Carmen booked a sitter twice a month to attend art museums, theater, and movies and go on hikes. They found other couples with small children and initiated family playdates. Through all these shared experiences, they strengthened their friendship and romance.

Tasha and Eric attended a marriage retreat they

found online that pushed them to talk about themselves individually and as a couple. They realized that they had not spent much time alone with each other in a very long time. The experience was awkward but eye-opening. They learned a lot about their relationship dynamic.

William and Kim started listening to music, rather than the television, at mealtimes. They asked each other, "How are you?" and pushed themselves to answer with more introspection, openness, and honesty. They set the intention to start touching more. They sat together on the couch, held hands, and kissed hello and goodbye. The physical intimacy in the bedroom improved.

Bruce and Carlos found a church that welcomed LGBTQ, and there they developed a community of friends. They got involved in community service projects and continued to share their love of food and wine. They frequented restaurants and started cooking together.

Keep motivated to continue the repair journey

Many couples state that the strongest motivations to repair their relationships are their children, friends, and finances. While these reasons may not sound very romantic, it is easy to recognize that one's primary relationship failure affects people and things outside of that partnership. Grasping the big picture of your affair's impact on others and your lifestyle can ignite a strong desire to do the hard work of healing and repair. Use the journal prompts to act on repairing your broken relationships.

I'm challenging you to embrace the following call to action: "I don't know precisely why I chose to have an affair, but I'm going to spend time looking deeper into my wrongdoing. I commit to this navel-gazing process to strengthen my empathy for those I have hurt and for myself. I will say out loud to myself and at least one other person what I'm discovering. Now and in the future, I will try my best to do what is right.

JOURNAL PROMPT
BUILDING INTIMACY

REFLECT ON YOUR PRIMARY RELATIONSHIP.

Emotional Intimacy

Do you openly share your feelings?

_____

_____

_____

_____

Possible Goal: Next week, talk for at least three minutes daily with your significant other, sharing one feeling you are experiencing.

Intellectual Intimacy

Do you discuss current events? Literature? Art?

_____

_____

_____

_____

Possible Goal: In the next week, talk for at least five minutes with your significant other about a topic of your choice (current events, literature, art).

Physical Intimacy

How often do you touch or show physical affection to your significant other? How satisfying is your sex life?

_____

_____

_____

_____

Possible Goal: In the next week, touch (hug, hold hands, massage, kiss) your significant other at least two times a day. With permission, initiate sexual contact once this week.

Experiential Intimacy

What activities do you and your significant other mutually enjoy?

_____

_____

_____

_____

Possible Goal: Plan a date night (dinner, theatre, a sporting event, hiking, etc.).

_____

Spiritual Intimacy

How willing are you to share your spiritual beliefs or sense of connection to something more significant than yourselves?

_____

_____

_____

_____

Possible Goal: Sit with your significant other and discuss your worldview, your religious beliefs, your belief in a higher power, or your thoughts about an afterlife. Discuss what you believe to be your life purpose. Be open in sharing your views and be curious as to theirs.

Now reflect on these five types of intimacies and how you connected with the other.

———

Make guesses as to why the two relationships were so different. Make guesses as to why YOU were different.

_____

_____

_____

_____

———

Say it OUT LOUD. Share your thoughts with a trusted friend or mental health professional.

COMMIT TO CHANGE

You have the power to turn the disaster of your affair into a tool for redemption. Are you committed to completely letting go of the secret life you led? Have you found meaning, stronger resolve, and determination to be a more loving and honest person? Recognize that you have a choice to grow and change, be more open, and commit to repairing your primary relationship. You may choose not to remain in your prior relationship. Listen to your inner wisdom and desires. Taking steps that others say you 'should' will be ineffective. The decision to deepen your apology is yours. If the intentions and goals you set for growth come from a place of sincerity and authenticity, they will be successful. What you hope for shapes your life priorities.

Fundamental transformation, strengthened by your honesty and humility, is visible to both you and others. Be aware of the myth of change. It is a falsehood to believe that simply "knowing better" will stop you from repeating your betrayal. The challenge is to behave differently in your relationships. Take actions that are morally driven and communicate a desire to be an open, honest person deserving of trust. What you do creates different energy, connections, credibility, emotions, and beliefs.

You are a work-in-progress. Every so often, think back to where you were two or three months earlier before you started *More Than Sorry*. Is your sense of self transforming? Be clear about your redemption goals and stick with them. Be patient if change comes slowly. Particularly, notice what repeating patterns in your life have shown up. Are the current mistakes redundant from any in the past? Continue to process your insights.

Carmen struggled with setting redemption goals. Initially defensive about changing anything more than stopping the intimate connection with her Facebook friend, she received clarity from online chat rooms that offered support, feedback, and a strong community of friends. Setting healthy boundaries built her confidence and self-respect. She also realized that she needed to reconnect with her music career to re-engage with her passions and expertise. She started to write songs and began teaching private piano and voice lessons to young people. Her redemption goals were to improve her self-care through healthy connections with others and creatively re-engage with her music. Carmen was then able to be fully present for Elena. Their relationship grew stronger through more in-depth sharing of their struggles, fears, and joys. Both were able to be more authentic and open with each other as their trust grew.

Staying committed to change is somewhat intellectual in that it is a decision. Have you committed to being different? Although life changes are inevitable, can you steer what is happening to meet your hopes and dreams? With clear redemption goals, you will determine the steps needed to ensure that the future does not repeat the past.

The motivation to transform can be both extrinsic and intrinsic. You may be extrinsically motivated by wanting others to see you positively, regain social status, and avoid divorce's financial burden. Hopefully, you also find intrinsic motivation to evolve inspired by your internal goals of compassion and self-respect. Listen to your heart and your head to drive growth inspired by your passion and desires. Continue your navel gazing to be aware of yourself and stay in touch with your emotions to energize your actions.

Bruce's love of Carlos motivated him to make changes. When traveling, he called home frequently and initiated intimate and open conversations. They learned more about each other, and their relationship grew more robust. Bruce also established better boundaries with co-workers and strengthened his sense of self-worth. Along with the external behavioral changes, he also worked on internal transformation, challenged his feelings of insecurity, and pushed himself to embrace his feelings of loneliness, boredom, and the need for ego strokes. Once he became more honest with himself, he gained more self-respect and inner peace. With his newfound authenticity, his connection with his partner became more intimate.

Tom wasn't ready to do honest navel gazing. He avoided self-exploration by diving back into his job, where he felt productive and respected. He wasn't willing to look at his marriage failures and at his choice to have an affair. His defensive mask was firmly in place, prohibiting him from making personal and relationship changes.

Tasha felt intense joy and excitement with the other and wasn't ready to accept that her choice to be romantically involved with another man was wrong. She felt little remorse for her affair but was unhappy that her infidelity damaged the cherished bond with extended family and friends, forcing a decision between continuing the relationship with the other or losing her community. Tasha worked to be more open, honest, and vulnerable to receive the support and intimacy she craved to regain trust and relationships with her extended family and friends.

Whether you stay with your partner or not, set a goal to be intentional about living openly, honestly, and authentically. Through this navel-gazing process, you have witnessed the truth of your betrayal. What looked like the end might just be the beginning. *A new season or chapter in your life has come, and it is one that you have the power to create.*

William and Kim started a ritual of "checking in," wherein he talked openly about his porn addiction, regressions, cravings, and successes. They did this weekly for a time, and consequently, Kim started to trust William again. Their connection became more honest and intimate. He realized how deeply he wanted to change and how passionately he wanted his marriage to survive. William has a sex addiction AND loves his wife and child. Tasha betrayed her husband, AND she is a good friend, caregiver, and grandparent. Bruce repeatedly cheated on Carlos AND is humble and committed to making change. Carmen had a hurtful online relationship, AND she is accepting her sin and making changes. Tom cheated on his wife, AND he is a generous community member devoted to his children and extended family.

You can find inner peace after the storm of an affair when you accept your duality. You sinned, AND you are responsible. You are, at times, selfish, AND you care deeply about others. You made bad choices, AND you are committing to making more loving choices from now on. Although the person you become tomorrow is not known, today's work will enhance your self-awareness and lead to healthier connections with others. Strive to evolve to be a better version of yourself. *Commit to becoming someone you respect when you look in the mirror.* What are your restitution goals?

After working with the journal prompts, move on to Step Five and ask for forgiveness.

I'm challenging you to embrace the following call to action: "I don't know exactly why I chose to have an affair, but I'm going to spend time looking deeper into my wrongdoing. I commit to this navel-gazing process to strengthen my empathy for those I have hurt and for myself. I will say out loud to myself and at least one other person what I'm discovering. Now, and in the future, I will try my best to do what is right."

JOURNAL PROMPT
COMMITTING TO CHANGE

Reflect on Alcoholic Anonymous serenity prayer: "God, grant me the serenity to accept the things I cannot change, the courage to change the things I can, and the wisdom to know the difference." Note what parts of you and your situation are unmovable and what pieces are open to transformation.

_____

_____

_____

_____

_____

Reflect on your energy and desire to commit to change.

_____

_____

_____

_____

_____

What are your transformation goals? In what ways do you hope to be different?

_____

_____

_____

_____

_____

What feedback have you received from the wounded, family, and friends about your changes?

_____

_____

_____

_____

"I accept my own dualities. I am both _____ AND
_____."

"I accept my own dualities. I am both _____ AND
_____."

"I accept my own dualities. I am both _____ AND
_____."

SAY IT OUT LOUD. SHARE YOUR THOUGHTS WITH A
TRUSTED FRIEND OR MENTAL HEALTH PROFESSIONAL.

STEP FIVE: ASK FOR FORGIVENESS

MOVE TOWARD FORGIVENESS

Y ou have heard the adage, "forgive and forget." The truth is the wounded, family, and friends will not forget your affair. Your extensive navel gazing will strengthen and re-energize relationships, and the intensity of the painful memories will fade with time. The possibility of being pardoned heightens as you continue to be more transparent and committed to living an open life. When you share your inner thoughts, feelings, and vulnerabilities, feel confident that trust will slowly build with those you have hurt.

The power of free choice.

The wounded and family's decision to take the journey to let go of their hurt, anger and mistrust is theirs and theirs alone. Instinctively, after a breach of trust, one will guard against future pain and disappointment, creating solid and protective walls. Accept that forgiveness is not an all-or-nothing or a black/white decision but has many shades of gray. Since there is no timeline for healing, don't make the mistake of insisting that enough time has passed post-affair and that the wounded should be "over it" at a time of your choosing.

Tom was impatient with Chloe. He felt smothered by her suspicion, questions, and mistrust. He insisted that enough time had been spent discussing his affair and wanted to move on. They grew more and more distant, had more arguments, and lost respect for each other. His resistance to navel gazing didn't help Chloe move toward forgiveness or repair their relationship.

Pray that the wounded and your family decide to let go of their deep resentment and anger and choose to forgive. Their decision to move toward forgiveness involves emotional, intellectual, relational, and spiritual choices. This path is multifaceted and complicated. Even with your best efforts to act on your restitution goals, the reality is that you can't completely fix the wounded's hurt and unhappiness. At some point in their healing, they must make a conscious choice to stop focusing on the betrayal and strive to imagine a different future that holds joy, security, and intimacy. (See "Tips for the Wounded" in Appendix A.)

The power of your actions.

Often your actions speak louder than your words. What you do and how you act matter. Do not passively sit and wishfully hope to be forgiven. Continue navel gazing.

- Share your thoughts and feelings.
- Put energy into the relationships you want to repair.
- Continue to communicate empathy and compassion to your loved ones.
- Genuinely demonstrate humility and remorsefulness.
- Apologize repeatedly.
- Acknowledge the guilt for your wrongdoings.

William loved Kim and wanted to move forward in their relationship. Realizing that his wife needed emotional support and practical help with the family, he strived to be more present. He continued to push himself to say out loud what he was thinking and feeling to build intimacy and connection. Even though there were positive signs that they were reconnecting, he had to let go of his need to hear Kim say, "I forgive you." She had to work through her fears, anger, and hurt before deciding what she wanted. William continued to be open and honest and hoped that his wife would move toward trust.

The power of self-forgiveness.

Forgiving oneself is also tricky. You can't erase your past transgressions, but you can stay grounded in the present with the commitment not to violate trust again. Accepting your weaknesses while taking steps to be different is challenging. Forgiving yourself includes owning the feelings of guilt, taking responsibility for your betrayal, and taking steps to remedy the situation you created. Remember the "and" discussed in the re-commit chapter? You sinned, and you have worked to repent. You are human – imperfect and valuable. *You are not "either/or," but the integration of weaknesses and your strengths.* With humility, start the path to self-forgiveness to improve your present and future relationships and strengthen your self-love.

William's shame tainted his porn addiction recovery. He was discouraged but continued to make changes – changes that were easier with Kim's support. Even with understanding his addiction, Kim could only let go of her anger and move to forgiveness after William did his recovery work in counseling and Sex Addicts Anonymous meetings.

The power of LIKE.

To re-energize your relationships, the wounded, your family, and you must learn to LIKE each other again. Affairs fuel resentment and cloud the love once felt for each other. Couples often state that they love their significant other but have fallen out of LIKE with them. Can you change this? Can you prove to the wounded that you are a trustworthy person, full of remorse and intent on being different? Can you be a better friend that is supportive, attentive, open, and reliable? Can you mutually shift your attitude and look at each other in a more positive light and with minor criticism? Can you let go of scorekeeping and resentment? Believe that the wounded and family all want the same thing as you – to love and like again with less pain and drama? With shared optimistic expectations, relationship repair is a realistic goal.

Eric chose to forgive Tasha. They had a long history of connection and respect that positively influenced them to start the next chapter of their relationship. Although they didn't stay married, mutual respect helped them to function successfully as parents and grandparents.

The power of forgiveness.

Forgiveness is the healthy balance between standing up to the betrayal, expecting restitution, and moving toward a joyful life. Management of the hurt requires putting it on the shelf periodically, out of the forefront of your mind, so that the flood of pain is manageable. Of course, individuals must regularly acknowledge their past trauma. Denial of past crisis is not healthy. But over time, carrying rage and pain leads to physical and emotional exhaustion, negatively impacting one's happiness, health, and relationships. Choosing to shed the heavy emotions of sadness and anger allows one to experience inner peace and reconnect with life's joys.

Bruce and Carlos were on the path to reconciliation. Carlos decided to forgive and to let go of the past. He started to trust that the one-night stands would not continue. While he continued to hold some suspicions, he chose to believe Bruce's stated intention to be different. Through forgiveness, they reconnected in a more vital, honest, and open way. With the weight of anger and hurt lifted, both no longer experienced sleepless nights, anxiety, and depression.

Over time, Elena chose to start the path to forgiveness. Even though she was disappointed by Carmen's secret relationship, she understood the boredom and isolation she felt. Elena saw how sincere her wife was in her efforts to make amends and reignite their partnership. Their post-affair relationship experienced a surge of intimacy, fun, and quality time that helped them let go of the past hurt and look, with hope, to the future.

The power of hope.

I know it's hard to continue this work with little promise of receiving complete or even partial forgiveness. It is crucial that you and those you have hurt hold on to hope for the next chapter in your current or future relationships. Accept that people change and that you can grow from the violation. Pray that the wounded and family will eventually let go of their hurt and anger. Strive to find inner peace and bask in the security of feeling loved and liked. If you choose to stay with the wounded, your relationship has the potential to be stronger and more intimate. If you decide to separate, respect yourself for the effort made and reflect on your personal growth, knowing that your future relationships will benefit from your navel gazing. Embrace the belief that this dark time in your life will pass and that your future will be different. *Inner peace is believing that today does not define tomorrow. Hold on to hope.*

Receiving forgiveness is liberating and truly is a gift. Are you ready to ask for forgiveness from your partner, family, friends, God, or a higher power, and yourself? Do you need to forgive anyone?

I'm challenging you to embrace the following call to action: "I don't know exactly why I chose to have an affair, but I'm going to spend time looking deeper into my wrongdoing. I commit to this navel-gazing process to strengthen my empathy for those I have hurt and for myself. I will say out loud to myself and at least one other person what I'm discovering. Now and in the future, I will try my best to do what is right."

MORE THAN SORRY

After your intensive navel gazing, it is time to write a sincere apology letter to your partner. You have processed your betrayal and hopefully have found the words to say more than "I'm sorry." The following are letters of apology written by Carmen, Bruce, Tom, and William after four months of navel gazing. As you read them, you will notice different levels of remorse, empathy, and requests for forgiveness. Use these examples to reflect on what you want to say in your apology letter.

Dear Elena,

I am so sorry for having an online relationship. I now know it was an affair – a secret relationship where I was obsessed and turned my back on you. I knew it was wrong in my gut, but I didn't want to acknowledge that I was cheating. It was too overwhelming to accept my betrayal. I selfishly tried to find happiness, mask my loneliness, and stuff down my guilt and shame. I realize that my character flaw is that I am easily swayed by others, neglecting to listen to my inner wisdom. I didn't want to be honest with myself – much less with you. I tried to escape from the loneliness of being a stay-at-home mom, and my new friend paid attention to me and flattered me. I didn't turn to you for support but to her. I didn't say out loud to you what I needed or how I felt, nor did I ask you how you were doing. I stepped over the line and betrayed you and blew your trust. I am genuinely sorry. I know I have hurt you, and I was selfish. And yet, you're trying to forgive me. Wow! After all the pain I've inflicted. I admire your generous, forgiving spirit.

Thank you for accepting me and all my flaws. I promise to say out loud what I need, do my own spiritual/moral work, listen to myself, and get more appropriate social connections. I love you and like you, and I will express it more. I am excited to reignite our passion and our friendship. I realize that the better I am at taking care of myself, the more authentically I will show up for us. I will continue to work hard in our relationship. I am grateful for being given a second chance. Already it feels like our time spent together is much more intimate. Thank you.

Love,
Carmen

One year later: Elena and Carmen stayed together. Their intimacy has deepened. Carmen continues to find appropriate community connections, improves her self-care, and engages in more joint activities.

Dear Carlos,

I now own up to my affairs and realize my moral code was terrible, and I'm genuinely embarrassed by my behavior. I was only interested in having fun and filling up my ego in such a disgusting way. I have discovered the broken place in me filled with fear and insecurity. Now, I will say NO. I pledge that I will not return to the double life I led. It embarrasses me when I realize how long I cheated and denied it to myself. I didn't justify it – I just didn't think about it. Now, I want to look in the mirror, respect who I am, respect the vow I made to you, and be honest, open, and faithful. I realize that my affairs tainted our relationship even though you didn't know what I was doing. I am sure you sensed a wall to our intimacy. While protecting my secrets, I could not be present with you, impacting our intimacy. I know we can be happy. I will work on being "good" individually by continuing to navel gaze. I love you, and I hope you will forgive me enough to continue to build a future together. Things will be different.

Love,

Bruce

One year later: Bruce and Carlos stayed together and started a ritual of asking each other, "How are you?" They have serious talks periodically to stay connected. They have built an exciting life together through various activities and are pursuing becoming parents.

Dear Chloe,

I am sorry that I hurt you and our family. I know that I

selfishly started an outside relationship without telling you and dealing with our marriage issues. I was not happy, and we had fallen into a cohabitating trap. Now, I am not sure what I want. I am not sure what you want. I promise to do a better job listening to your pain and desires, and I hope you will reciprocate. I do know that we will forever be tied together as we parent our children. I hope we can deal with those responsibilities without resentment and anger.

Tom

One year later: Tom and Chloe got divorced. She couldn't forgive or trust him again because she didn't feel his navel gazing was sincere. He admitted that he was not fully committed to reconciling their differences. Their struggle with mutual respect currently interferes with their ability to work together as parents.

Dear Kim,

After navel gazing, I know that I have a problem – a problem with porn. I know that I need to go to Sex Addict meetings and therapy regularly to be more focused and intentional about changing. I know that I need to manage my stress and anxiety and find more joy in our life together. As you know, I have had little relationship experience. You are my first real commitment. I know that I love you, and I am so sorry that I have hurt you and our finances with my secrets. I know that I need to be more present in our marriage and spend more time with you and the kids. I hope you'll forgive me and help support me as I work on myself. I truly feel your love for me and your desire for us to work things out. I think we both need to ask for help more often. I want to be there for you, too. I hope I can be the husband that you deserve.

Love,
William

One year later: William and Kim stayed together and continued to attend therapy. He has had relapses with his use of pornography but gets support from the SAA community.

Dear Eric,

I am sorry that I disappointed and hurt you and the family with my affair. I am sure you felt blindsided. I know we were in a complacency rut, and I wasn't turning to you as my husband. I realize that I was playing the martyr and not asking for help or saying out loud how I felt. I thought you wouldn't care if I stayed with you. I didn't ask or expect you to support me as I struggled with loneliness, boredom, and unhappiness. I took the easy way out by starting the affair. It was initially fun and an escape. I don't want to be "that woman" who abandons her family for purely selfish reasons. I hate hurting so many of our family members. My friends who have extended grace, love, and forgiveness are amazing. You and I have a lot of work to do to see if forgiveness and reconnection can occur. I am committed to more therapy and talk, and exploration of what we want for our future.

Tasha

One year later: Tasha and Eric ended their marriage. They are still friends and are comfortable sharing family time and holidays.

JOURNAL PROMPT
ASK FOR FORGIVENESS

Write apology letters to:

1. Your partner
2. Your family
3. Your friends
4. God or your higher power
5. Yourself

How will you handle it if the wounded and family aren't ready to forgive?

_____

_____

_____

_____

_____

What do you need or want to hear from the wounded or family?

_____

_____

_____

_____

_____

Do you need to forgive anyone?

_____

_____

_____

_____

_____

SAY IT **OUT LOUD.** SHARE YOUR THOUGHTS WITH A TRUSTED FRIEND OR MENTAL HEALTH PROFESSIONAL.

PERSONAL AND RELATIONAL GROWTH CONTINUES

LOOKING BACK AND LOOKING FORWARD

Congratulations! You have completed the five steps to deepen your apology for your infidelity. You practice empathy, show compassion for those you have hurt, have learned more about who you are, and set goals for transformation. After an intense navel-gazing process, you demonstrate the courage to own your transgression, sharing openly with others. You have sincerely apologized to those hurt by your infidelity and are willing to answer the question, "Why did I have an affair?".

Your betrayal is part of who you are, but not ALL of who you are. You bore witness to your bad choices, and perhaps you have committed to being different – to repent. From your newfound transparency and authenticity, you can now experience a more vital peace of mind and deeper intimacy in relationships.

Your navel gazing journey does not end with this chapter. Embrace the lifelong journey of being empathetic, self-discovery, sharing out loud with others your inner world, committing to personal growth and change, admitting your wrongdoings, and asking for forgiveness. Continue to write your redemption story and trust that you and your relationships can change. "Before and after" are opposites that don't cancel each other out. Integrate your past transgression with a firm resolve to not lead a secret life again. Accept the magnitude of your betrayal and frequently revisit your best guesses as to why you crossed the line and broke the trust in your relationship. It may feel redundant to keep looking back, but your answer will change with time and increased self-awareness. *Simply put, you are the author of a life that was sinful, and now you are on the road to gaining respect.*

Have clarity about your accomplishments and the steps taken toward future growth. Look in the mirror and respect that you are a flawed human who takes responsibility for their transgressions and set redemption goals. You are now more honest, and your public, private, and secret selves are open for all to see.

Celebrate all your ah-ha's and self-discoveries. New seasons in your relationships are on the horizon. Regaining trust is tenuous, and the work to maintain healthy relationships has no end date. I encourage couples to regularly schedule "check-ins" to discuss their relationship and share inner thoughts and feelings OUT LOUD. Simply ask:

- "How do you think we are doing as a couple?"
- "What residues from the affair are we still struggling with?"
- "What should we be working on now as a couple?"

- "Today, when I reflect on my affair, I
  think/feel..."
- If you are not in the same relationship with
  the wounded, continue to "check-in" with
  yourself and ask:
- "How has my affair impacted who I am today?"
- "Today, when I reflect on my affair, I
  think/feel..."

Have faith that you can be a better, more honest person who has a life filled with joy and meaning. The reward from completing *More Than Sorry* is realizing that change can happen. I applaud your tenacity and your commitment to creating a better life after your affair.

After stepping up to the many "calls to action" presented in this book, you can now say: "I know more about 'why' I chose to have an affair. I will continue to deepen my apology through honest self-awareness and exploration while intentionally setting goals for self-improvement. I recognize that my choices impact others and affect the quality of my relationships. Now and in the future, I will try my best to do what is right."

JOURNAL PROMPT

WHY? REVISIT THE QUESTION OF WHY YOU HAD A SECRET
RELATIONSHIP

Today, my answer to: "Why? Why did I have a secret
relationship?" is...

_____

_____

_____

Today, my redemption story that reflects the change,
healing, and new beginnings is:

_____

_____

_____

S AY IT OUT LOUD. S HARE YOUR THOUGHTS WITH A
TRUSTED FRIEND OR MENTAL HEALTH PROFESSIONAL.

JOURNAL PROMPT
REVIEWING THE FIVE STEPS TO DEEPEN YOUR APOLOGY

Communicating Empathy:

In the past few days, have you validated the thoughts and feelings of those you wounded? Do you verbalize remorse for the hurt you have inflicted? Do you show compassion to others and yourself? Have you acknowledged your frustrations and successes? Note that communicating empathy needs to be repeated frequently.

_____

_____

_____

_____

_____

_____

_____

_____

Self-Discovery:

How often have you tuned into your inner voice and processed your thoughts and emotions with others or through journaling in the past few days? What coping mechanisms are you utilizing when dealing with frustrations? Are you honest about your strengths and failings? Do you continue to process why you chose to have an affair?

_____

_____

_____

_____

_____

_____

_____

Say it Out Loud:

How often are you honestly sharing reflections of your affair, the status of your current relationships, and your self-discovery journey with a confidante? Do you talk more openly with those you have betrayed?

_____

_____

_____

_____

_____

_____

_____

Restitution Goals:

How transparent are your dreams for personal and relational growth? What steps have you recently taken to pursue these goals?

_____

_____

_____

_____

_____

_____

_____

Ask for Forgiveness:

Have you written a letter or offered a deepened apology for your infidelity to those impacted by your actions?

_____

_____

_____

_____

_____

_____

_____

_____

APPENDIX A

TIPS FOR THE WOUNDED

How are you? Understandably, the shock and the pain from the betrayal are horrific. Hopefully, you are getting more answers to "WHY?" as your significant other works at navel gazing. As time passes, the expectation is that you will find peace, let go of wanting to know more about the betrayal, and let go of replaying all of the scenes of the affair that are stuck in your head. But don't passively wait for time to erase the pain. Actively work at your navel gazing.

Here are some tips for moving on and letting go:

- You get to bring up the affair. I suggest you bring it up by saying, "I was thinking about your affair today. It was a hard day for me. I feel sad/angry/relieved (whatever you feel)." Share your emotions of the day with no need to rehash the whole situation again. The hope is that your intimacy and closeness will increase with saying thoughts and feelings out loud.

- Ask for reassurance. Ask for hugs. Ask to hear, "I'm sorry," again and as often as you need.
- You need to listen. Challenge yourself to listen with curiosity and without deflecting with comments like, "Yes, BUT…"
- Give yourself breaks from the intense conversations. You can't talk about this 24-hours a day, seven days a week.
- Continue the routines of life taking care of home, family, and work.
- Exercise.
- Pray and or meditate.
- Schedule fun activities.
- Be compassionate to yourself. Don't judge your mood swings and emotional blow-ups. You must embrace the roller coaster of healing.
- Can you find compassion for the navel gazer? That doesn't mean allowing him/her to be off the hook for the offense. Maybe you can dive deeper into the motivation and significance of the secret relationship. Mutually, you can explore the "Why?" of the affair.
- Consider how resilient you are. Can you bounce back? Can you look for how to be different, maybe individually and as a couple?
- Talk, talk, talk. Say your thoughts and feelings out loud. The goal is to achieve intimacy by

discussing your emotions, needs, and future dreams.

- You get to decide what will happen in your relationship. Trust the process. You may not know what you want right now. Take your time.
- You need to get support from a therapist or a trusted friend/family member to whom you can communicate your pain.
- Whether or not you stay in the relationship, finding some level of forgiveness will help you feel more at peace. Forgiveness is not saying that the affair was okay. Forgiveness allows you to let go of the past (not the memories) and look to healthier relationships in the future. Forgiveness will be easier if you feel like the offender is genuinely remorseful and accepting of their betrayal and the pain the affair inflicted on others.
- The goal is to eventually tell the story of this secret relationship in a way that frames it as a dark time that led to a healthier and more intimate relationship. The affair is part of your relationship story, but not the whole story. How will you write your recovery story?

APPENDIX B

Dear Therapist,

I am encouraging you to partner with your client in their naval gazing. I recommend you follow *More Than Sorry*'s blueprint and provide a safe place for the cheater to share their affair story. Utilizing your training in the power of communicating unconditional, positive regard will support the integration of past transgressions with current work of expanding awareness, authenticity, and honesty. Saying "out loud" all that has happened will encourage personal and relational growth, self-awareness, confession, change, and perhaps forgiveness.

As therapists, we all have our biases. You may have strong feelings about infidelity. You may have experienced it personally. If you work with couples, you have very likely dealt with it professionally. It is tempting to take sides and support the victim and demonize the offender. I'm sure that you know that such bias only creates more silence and withdrawal and flares anger and woundedness in both the individuals and the relationship.

Beware of a fixing mentality. As therapists, we can't erase the past or promise a happy future. We can't control or determine which couples will stay together and which ones won't. Accept that this is the client's journey and decision to repair or end their partnership. I am confident that you will encourage the adulterer's self-examination and teach the skills of validation and empathy. Your therapeutic role is to act as a mirror to help the client see themself more clearly and honestly. With this reflection, they will be able to determine desires and steps toward personal and relational change.

I am hopeful that this resource will strengthen your work with individuals and couples. Therapeutic repair after infidelity is a combination of couple's work and individual sessions.

I would love to hear about your work. Feel free to contact me.

Dr. Deborah Miller
Licensed Professional Counselor
drdebmiller@drdebmiller.com

BIBLIOGRAPHY

Allouche, Kim Sutton. "You've Got Mail! A Cyber Relationship Sparks New Discovery". Psychotherapy Networker (March/April 2011): 77-80.

Ariely, Dan. "Our Buggy Moral Code". Filmed February 2009 at TED2009. Retrieved from: http:www.ted.com/talks/ dan_ariely_our_buggy_ moral_code.

Baptiste, Baron. Being of Power: The 9 Practices to Ignite an Empowered Life. California: Hay House, 2013.

Brackett, Marc, Ph.D. Permission to Feel: Unlocking the Power of Emotions to Help Our Kids, Ourselves, and Our Society Thrive. New York: Celadon Books, 2019.

Brown, Brene. "Rising Strong: How the Ability to Reset Transforms the Way We Live, Love Parent, and Lead. New York: Spiegel & Grau, 2017.

Cameron, Julia. The Artist's Way. New York: Tarcher/Putnam, 2002.

Casarjian, Robin. Forgiveness: A Bold Choice for a Peaceful Heart. New York: Bantam Books, 1992.

Chapman, Gary. The Five Love Languages: How to Express Heartfelt Commitment to Your Mate. Northfield: Chicago, 2004

Cohen-Posey, Kate. Brief Therapy Client Handouts. New York: Wiley & Sons, 2000.

Dodgson, Lindsay. "These are the 3 types of attachment styles- and how each affects your relationships". Retrieved from http://Insider.com (June 13, 2018).

Enright, Robert D. Forgiveness is a Choice: A Step-by-Step Process for Resolving Anger and Restoring Hope. Washington, D.C.: American Psychological Association, 2011.

Fisher, Helen. "Why we Love, Why We Cheat". Filmed at TED2006. Retrieved at http.www. ted.com/talks/helen_fisher_tells_us_why_we_ love_cheat.

Gilbert, Dan. "The Psychology of your Future Self." Ted Talk. Filmed at TED2014.http.www. ted.com/talks/dan_gilbert_you_ are_always_changing.

Glass, Shirley P. Not "Just Friends": Rebuilding Trust and Recovering Your Sanity After Infidelity. New York: Free Press, 2003.

Gottman, John, and Julie. "The Science of Togetherness". Psychotherapy Networker. (Sept/Oct 2017): 44-47.

Hill, Tamara "Self-Forgiveness: 7 Ways We Block Personal Growth". 1/20/14. Retrieved at: http:// blogs.psychcentral.com/caregivers/2013/12/self-forgiveness

Howes, Ryan. "Brave New Couples: What can Science Tell us About the Changing Face of Couplehood Today?" Interview with Susan Johnson. Psychotherapy Networker, May/June 2015.

Marshall, Andrew G. Why Did I Cheat? Help Your
Partner (and Yourself) Recover from Your
Affair. Marshall Method Publishing, 2019.

Melton, Glennon Doyle. Carry On, Warrior: The
Power of Embracing Your Messy, Beautiful
Life. New York: Scribner, 2013.

Mitrokostas, Sophia. "Here's What Happens to
your Body and Brain When You Orgasm".
Business Insider, January 26, 2019.

Myss, Caroline. Archetypes: A Beginner's Guide to
Your Inner-net. Carlsbad, California: Hays
House, 2013.

Nelson, Tammy. The New Monogamy: Redefining
Your Relationship After Infidelity. Oakland:
New Harbinger, 2012.

Perel, Esther. The State of Affairs: Rethinking
Infidelity. New York: HarperCollins
Publishers, 2017.

Perel, Esther. "Couples Therapy for Moving Past
Affairs". Psychotherapy Networker, 9/2/15.

Perel, Esther. "The Secret to Desire in a Long-
Term Relationship". Filmed February 2013 at
TEDSalon, New York, NY. Retrieved from:
www.ted.com/talks/

esther_perel_the_secret_to_
desire_in_a_long_term_relationship.

Perel, Esther. "Rethinking Infidelity...a Talk for
anyone who has ever Loved". Filmed May 2015
TED.com. Retrieved from; https://www.ted.
com/
talks/esther_perel_rethinking_infidelity_a_talk
_for_anyone_who_has_ever_loved

Pittman, Frank. Private Lies: Infidelity & the
Betrayal of Intimacy. New York: Norton, 1989.

Poppink, Joanna MFT. Healing Your Hungry
Heart: Recovering From your Eating disorder.
San Francisco: Conari Press, 2011.

Prager, Joshua, "In Search of the Man Who Broke
my Neck". Filmed at TED 2013. https:www.ted.
com/talks/joshua_prager_in_search
_for_the_man_who_broke_my_neck.

Rich, P. & Schwartz, L.L. The healing Journey
Through Divorce: Your Journal of
Understanding and Renewal. New York: John
Wiley and Sons, 1999.

Spring, Janis. A. How Can I forgive you? The
Courage to Forgive, the Freedom Not to. New
York: Harper, 2004.

Warren, Rick. The Purpose Driven Life: What On Earth Am I Here For? Grand Rapids, MI: Zondervan, 2012.

Weiner-Davis, Michele. Healing from Infidelity. Woodstock, IL: Michele Weiner-Davis Training Corporation, 2017.

Whyte, David. "In Search of the Big Story: Learning to ask the Beautiful Questions". Psychotherapy Networker, January/February 2016.

Williamson, Marianne. A Return to Love: Reflections on the Principles of a Course in Miracles. New York: HarperPerennial, 1992.

NOTES

Repair Your Broken Relationships

1. Chapman, Gary (2004). The Five Love Languages: How to Express Heartfelt Commitment to Your Mate. Northfield: Chicago.

ABOUT THE AUTHOR

 Deborah Miller, Ed.D. is a licensed professional counselor in private practice for over 20 years. As a trained Gestalt therapist, she works with a wide range of clients and concerns. She provides therapy for adults, children, adolescents, and their families. For the last 15 years of practice as a therapist, her focus is heavy on post-affair recovery. She helps couples increase intimacy, regain trust, and encourages them to like each other again.

Before being a mental health practitioner, Deborah worked for over 25 years in education as a counselor, a special education teacher, an administrator, a prevention/intervention specialist, and a visiting university professor. She conducted multiple workshops, nationally and internationally, for students and adults on strategies to support positive mental health.

Deborah is also proud that she and her husband have celebrated over 40 years of marriage. They survive life's roller coaster through the practice of navel gazing.

ACKNOWLEDGMENTS

More Than Sorry could not have happened without the support of so many people. Friends, colleagues, and family always showed interest and encouragement in this project over the years. Ironically, the COVID-19 pandemic gave me space and time to write and pursue the dream of publishing. Meghan Hill, a fantastic editor, and cheerleader offered her expertise and much-needed direction. Self-Publishing School, founded by Chandler Bolt, showed up in my life at the perfect time. Through the curriculum, coaching, and SPS Facebook community, I found inspiration and information. My SPS coach, Brett Hilker, was instrumental in bringing this book to fruition through his spot-on feedback and expansive understanding of the self-publishing world.

My family, including Mark, Katie, Danielle, and Ethan, offered much-needed feedback and encouragement. Dr. Marcus Ryan Miller, my son, served as my accountability partner as well as an editor.

Of course, I acknowledge all the clients I have worked

with over the past decades. The privilege of sitting through their journeys to heal from betrayal has inspired *More Than Sorry*. Without these shared experiences, I would have little to offer to those struggling with the aftermath of a betrayal.

I am grateful to all who played a role in helping *More Than Sorry; Five Steps to Deepen Your Apology After You Have Committed Infidelity*. It took a village!

I am very appreciative of you, the reader!

I look forward to you feedback and will use your reactions to shape my future work.

I hope you will take the time to leave an honest review on Amazon.

Thank you very much!

Dr. Deborah Miller

Made in the USA
Las Vegas, NV
08 December 2021